"Paul Turner offers us a concise and accessible guide to the post–Vatican II eucharistic liturgy, replete with a great deal of historical information. This book should provide an excellent guide for parish liturgy committees and anyone interested in gaining a fuller understanding of what we do when we come together for Eucharist."

— John F. Baldovin, SJ
Boston College School of Theology and Ministry

"Using the question 'Whose Mass is it?' Paul Turner uncovers the skein of relationships that give people, from the local sacristan to the curial officials of the Congregation for Divine Worship and Discipline of the Sacraments, a sense of ownership of the Mass. The number of stakeholders is more than most of us imagine, and the relationships between stakeholders are not always easy. Turner invites each stakeholder to recognize the others. He acknowledges the challenges brought on by change, conflicts won and lost, familial tensions heightened—and sometimes resolved—and gifts many and varied shared, neglected, or rejected. With great scholarly erudition and even greater pastoral wisdom, Turner charts a path of mutual recognition that invites each of us to recognize that the liturgy ultimately belongs to Christ, the center who holds both the liturgy and all of us together."

— Bernadette Gasslein
Editor, *Worship*

D1606660

Whose Mass Is It?

Why People Care So Much about the Catholic Liturgy

Paul Turner

LITURGICAL PRESS

Collegeville, Minnesota

www.litpress.org

1   2   3   4   5   6   7   8   9

Library of Congress Cataloging-in-Publication Data

Turner, Paul, 1953–
     Whose Mass is it? : why people care so much about the Catholic liturgy / Paul Turner.
          pages cm
     ISBN 978-0-8146-4867-4 — ISBN 978-0-8146-4892-6 (ebook)
          1. Mass—History—20th century.   2. Catholic Church—Liturgy—History—20th century.   3. Liturgical movement—Catholic Church—History—20th century.   I. Title.

     BX2230.3.T88   2015
     264'.02036—dc23

                                                                    2015012004

MICHÆLI ET CAROLÆ MATHEWS

GRATIAS AGIT AVCTOR

PROPTER PARTICIPATIONEM

PLENAM, CONSCIAM, ACTVOSAMQVE EORVM

IN MISSA, MENSA

ET RECREATIONE SVA

Contents

Acknowledgments

I wish to thank
Hans Christoffersen, who pitched,
Jaroslav Pelikan, who won,
Ernie Davis, Sheila Dierks, Carmel Pilcher, Paul Taylor, and
    Archbishop Dominic Jala, who coached,
Michael Joncas, who analyzed,
Gordon Lathrop and David Holeton, who visited,
and God, who keeps score.

PT

Introduction

Vested and ready for Mass to begin, the other altar servers and I swapped jokes and then stepped into the dark. We hurried from our sacristy to the priests' sacristy through the narrow, dim corridor that stretched unseen behind the high altar of St. Therese Church. It was the mid-1960s. We emerged from that cramped space into the bright room where two of our priests were discussing furniture.

Crowding the priests' sacristy was a tall, spindly wooden table. I'd never seen it before.

An odd thought occurred to me. I decided to say it out loud because it seemed outlandish at the time. From inside the priests' sacristy, I pointed toward the sanctuary.

"We could put this table out there, and the priest could stand behind it during Mass!"

The two priests looked at each other. Then at me.

"Well," one of them said, "that's exactly what we're planning to do."

Adult Catholics love the Mass for the same reason that young Catholics struggle with it. It's predictable. Repeated patterns ease adults into prayer. Repetition bores youth.

When the routine changes, everyone has an opinion. Today if I nudge the presider's chair to a different angle, I may encounter honest questions, irate parishioners, or reports to the bishop. When change happens higher up—at the national or global level—erudition, misunderstanding, and hysteria all vie for attention.

Whether or not adult Catholics attend Mass regularly, they strongly bond with it. If something has changed since the last time they participated, it threatens their very identity. Comfortable with what they know, Catholics are not so comfortable with the unfamiliar.

During the development of the 2011 revised English translation of the Roman Missal, the familiar was undergoing change. People gradually became aware that someone else's decision was going to affect the cornerstone of their spiritual life. Many voices rose to support or oppose the project. Opinions crystallized around the quality of the translation, the process for its advance, and the true place of authority in the church. The strength, diversity, and sweep of these opinions uncovered the intense relationship between individual Catholics and the community's Mass.

Within a single generation, English-speaking Catholics had experienced the Second Vatican Council's authorization for the first overhaul of the liturgy in four hundred years and then a revised vernacular translation. Each of these two events awakened strong feelings. An outside observer, watching Catholics jostle positions and parry apologetics, must have wondered, "Whose Mass is it?"

1

The Mass after the
Second Vatican Council

The Consilium

Many Catholics give a common answer to this question: "What were the two biggest changes to the Mass after the Second Vatican Council?" Especially for those who lived through those changes, the consensus would be clear: "Mass is in English, and the priest faces the people."

Neither of those changes precisely appears in the council's landmark Constitution on the Sacred Liturgy from 1963.[1] Nevertheless, they developed early and naturally from its principles. The council extended the limits of the vernacular languages at Mass, in the sacraments, and in other areas of the liturgy. It listed several elements of worship as examples, including "some"—not all—of the prayers and chants.[2] Once people experienced the changes, however, the very bishops who approved the liturgical constitution at the council advocated further expanding the use of vernacular.

The option for the priest to face the people from behind a freestanding altar first appeared nine months after the Constitution on the Sacred Liturgy, as part of an instruction for implementing its liturgical norms: "The main altar should preferably be freestanding, to permit walking around it and celebration facing the people. Its location in the place of worship should be truly central so that the attention of the whole congregation naturally focuses there."[3]

These two changes, then, which probably seemed small and logical at the time, made the greatest impact on the Catholic faithful. More than any other change, the use of vernacular languages and the placement of the altar brought life to the council's call for the full, conscious, active participation of the people. They also demonstrated ways that the theories within the council's liturgical constitution had to be elaborated into practice. As will be seen, however, they assumed a eucharistic theology of participation that neither clergy nor laity have fully grasped.

To carry out the vision of the liturgical renewal approved by the council, Pope Paul VI established a group of specialists known as the Consilium for Implementing the Constitution on the Sacred Liturgy. The pope did not hand the task to his curia; he appointed this separate commission. Nonetheless, the Consilium's first instruction, *Inter œcumenici*, which included the instruction on the freestanding altar, was approved by the curia's Sacred Congregation of Rites.

The Consilium organized dozens of study groups staffed by relevant experts. These groups proposed revisions to the immense library of liturgical celebrations—baptisms and funerals, weddings and ordinations, the Divine Office and the Mass. And more. The liturgical year, the Mass of chrism, the lectionary. It took several of these study groups to revise the Mass. In some cases, the groups sent their preliminary work to select pastoral centers around the world for experimentation and commentary. All the study groups submitted reports back to the Consilium, which revised them and submitted them to the Congregation of Rites and the pope for approval. Thus, the Catholic liturgy was reborn.

Changing the language of the people's parts of the Mass and the position of the priest encapsulated the changes that Catholics experienced; however, many did not grasp the significant changes to the Order of Mass, the words and actions that repeat with each celebration. People were somewhat unfamiliar with the details of the flow of the Mass because the priest had been using a low voice to speak most of his lines in Latin with his back to the people. The structural changes went largely unnoticed because of the very factors people did notice: the language and the position of the priest. Decades later, people still refer to the Mass before Vatican II as "the Latin Mass"—as if the postconciliar Mass is simply a verbal translation of the preconciliar one. But much more had happened.

The sign of the cross at the start of Mass became a dialogue between the priest and the people. The prayers at the foot of the altar were simplified into the revised penitential act. The occasions for singing the Gloria were minimized. The Sunday readings were expanded from a one-year cycle of two readings (an epistle and a gospel) into a three-year cycle of three readings, offering an extensive array of Old Testament passages for the first time. The Apostles' Creed became an option to the Nicene Creed. The universal prayer (the prayer of the faithful) was restored after centuries of disuse. The procession of the gifts was introduced; the priest thus no longer had the bread on the altar from the beginning of Mass. The "offertory" morphed into the "preparation of the gifts"; this change reserved the language about "offering" for the eucharistic prayer, while it introduced a new dialogue to clarify the preparatory purpose of this part of the Mass. Pre-consecration prayers that referred to the "spotless host" and the "saving cup" were removed. The number of prefaces multiplied. Nine eucharistic prayers were added to the single one formerly in use, and the people were encouraged to pray silently together with the priest. The people received a memorial acclamation to sing after the consecration. Multiple signs of the cross were removed from the eucharistic prayer, including those that the priest made near the end of the prayer over the consecrated elements, as if he were blessing the Body and Blood of Christ. The Lord's Prayer, which the priest had been praying alone and silently, was given to the entire assembly to offer together aloud. The prayers leading up to Communion were rearranged for a better flow. The sign of peace among the faithful was restored as an option. The faithful were allowed opportunities for Communion under both forms. The concluding rites were simplified so that the Mass ended with the dismissal of the faithful into the world. People who think that the post–Vatican II Mass is simply a vernacular translation of the pre–Vatican II Latin Mass are missing the many points of revision that brought the purpose of the Eucharist into clearer light.

The dynamics also changed. Participation at Mass prior to the council had been primarily an opportunity for private prayer executed at a common place and time. Since the council, people are expected to participate throughout the liturgy with common words, postures, and actions. Worshipers are to pay attention to the same words at the same time, so that the community prays the entire Mass as one.

These and other changes to the Order of Mass were elaborated by one of the study groups reporting to the Consilium.[4] They demonstrated that the church had the authority to change elements of the Mass. The Mass does not belong to some idealized past; it belongs to the living church.

Presidential Prayers

Nonetheless, the past has a voice. Most of the pages of the Roman Missal contain sets of three presidential prayers: the collect, the prayer over the offerings, and the prayer after communion. The presiding priest sings or says these, and all the people answer "Amen." Each prayer lasts only a few seconds, and many priests and people pay them scant attention; however, they interweave a library of resources from various times and traditions of church history. They expand the view of whose Mass it is that the community celebrates.

The three principal sources are sacramentaries called the Verona, the Gelasian, and the Gregorian. They were compiled in the sixth, seventh, and eighth centuries, respectively, and they preserved some prayers that are even older. The Roman Missal today retains many of these orations in positions similar to their original setting. For example, the prayer over the offerings for the Christmas Vigil Mass comes word for word from one of the Christmas prayers in the sixth-century Verona Sacramentary. The collects for the three scrutiny Masses that are usually observed during Lent are lifted from the same three occasions in the Gelasian Sacramentary. The collect for the Third Sunday in Ordinary Time, which unfailingly falls a few weeks after New Year's, first appeared in the Gregorian Sacramentary's prayers for a Sunday in January.[5]

Thus, the revised liturgy believes that older prayers should be preserved when possible. The Missal does not retain every prayer from every medieval sacramentary, but it keeps many of them. In addition, some ancient sources that the previous missal had never mined contributed to the postconciliar missal's library of prayers. For example, the collect for the Third Sunday of Advent now comes from the Rotulus of Ravenna, a fifth- to sixth-century collection of prayers that had been lost but was rediscovered in the nineteenth century. The collect formerly in use on that day has been replaced because the one from the Rotulus captures the spirit of joy in the day's popular name, *Gaudete* Sunday.

Some postconciliar prayers were imported from the Ambrosian Rite. Before his election, Pope Paul VI had been the cardinal archbishop of Milan, where the Ambrosian Rite is centered. The collects for the Thirteenth, Sixteenth, and Nineteenth Sundays in Ordinary Time, for example, were all copied from the Ambrosian Rite's Bergamo Sacramentary. They had never before appeared in a Roman missal.

Some ancient prayers were composed explicitly to defend church teachings against heresies. For example, dualistic Manichaeans believed that all matter was evil and only spiritual beings were good. The Christian belief that the invisible God became human seemed incomprehensible to Manichaeans: if matter is evil, why would a spiritual being take on human form? The Verona Sacramentary includes a collect for Christmas that may have been written by Pope Leo the Great in defense of the Christian position. It acknowledges the dignity of human nature, which God made even greater through the incarnation. Paul VI's Consilium added this ancient collect to the postconciliar missal in order to replace a less expressive prayer at the Christmas Mass During the Day. It also supplied the context for the prayer that the priest says at every Mass when he adds water to the wine: when he prays that "we may come to share in the divinity of Christ who humbled himself to share in our humanity," he is quoting this same prayer for Christmas Day. Even though the Manichaeans are long gone, the collect has reappeared in the postconciliar missal, probably because of its authorship, influence, beauty, and antiquity.

Similarly, one section of the Roman Canon supported Christian belief against the Manichaeans. The core of the Canon came to light in the fourth century, but it underwent subsequent additions and revisions all the way into the twentieth century. The section in question refers to the bread and wine offered by Melchizedek as "a holy sacrifice, a spotless victim." That line was added during the days of Leo the Great, contemporaneous with the aforementioned Christmas prayer. It affirms that even in their natural state, bread and wine have a sanctity and beauty that makes them eligible as an offering to God. Again, probably due to the antiquity of the Roman Canon, the phrase remains in the postconciliar missal's first eucharistic prayer. In a completely different and postmodern context unforeseen by the Consilium, these anti-Manichaean phrases should delight those who hold a neo-Teilhardian belief in the sacredness of the entire cosmos.[6]

In some cases, ancient prayers were deliberately reworked for contemporary sensibilities. For example, the prayer for the Jews on Good Friday has been completely redrafted. From the seventh to the twentieth centuries, the Catholic faithful who gathered on Good Friday prayed for the conversion of the Jews. Even before the Second Vatican Council, the language of this prayer referring to the "blindness" of the Jews had been removed. The revisers of the postconciliar missal, however, gave this petition an entirely new purpose, inspired by the council's more enlightened view of interreligious dialogue: that the Jewish people may attain the fullness of redemption.

The Gelasian Sacramentary, the source for that Good Friday prayer, also contained a Mass for dedicating a former synagogue as a Christian church. This Mass could have been composed because of a frequent need or because of a single instance after which the prayers were gathered up along with those composed for other unrelated circumstances, lest the work be lost. The collect revealed the same prejudice against the Jewish people found in the Good Friday prayer. Although that Mass has long been excluded from the Missal, its prayer after communion is assigned to the Thirty-Second Sunday in Ordinary Time. Its intention is so generic—that the grace of integrity may endure—that its origins are completely obscured. Still, one wonders why someone in the Consilium's study group was surveying that part of the Gelasian Sacramentary for inspiration. The council approved the retention of many ancient prayers, but not the retention of ancient prejudices.

Some presidential prayers are hybrids of older ones. For example, the collect for the Third Sunday of Easter took elements from a prayer over the people in the Gelasian Sacramentary and a prayer for the dead in the Verona Sacramentary. The resulting oration is entirely new to the post–Vatican II Mass, but it has ancient sources.

Some prayers are totally new compositions. For example, a Vigil Mass for the Ascension was added to the third edition of the Roman Missal in 2002. The prayer after communion was composed for the occasion. It could be heard in English for the first time ever when the revised translation made it available for the solemnity of the Ascension in 2012.

The contents of the Missal were prepared primarily by the Consilium's study groups, confirmed by the curia, and approved by Paul VI. As the Missal went into its second and third editions, however, other unnamed scholars made further emendations. All those involved retained elements from preconciliar editions of the Missal and from sources even older, while they developed the composition of some entirely new prayers in the style of their predecessors. One could argue that the Mass belongs to a postconciliar church, but antiquity still has a voice.

On a more practical level, the priest who presides often has a choice of prayers to use, especially on weekdays of Ordinary Time.[7] Furthermore, at Masses with a large number of children, he may choose alternative presidential prayers more suitable to children, preferably from the same liturgical season of the year, and he may simplify their wording for ease of comprehension.[8] Otherwise, the priest is not supposed to vary the words or swap the prayers—though, in practice, some do. Still, the Mass belongs to the entire Church, not just to the priest. Some of the prayers literally belong to the ages.

Eucharistic Prayer II

Almost all the eucharistic prayers are postconciliar compositions. Eucharistic Prayer III was entirely created by the Consilium's study group responsible for the Order of Mass. Eucharistic Prayer IV shares some affinity with the Anaphora of St. Basil but is another new composition. The three Eucharistic Prayers for Masses with Children, the one for Masses for Various Needs and Occasions (in four versions), and the two Eucharistic Prayers for Masses of Reconciliation were all newly written after the council.

The Missal's first two eucharistic prayers have ancient sources but appear in revision. The changes to the postconciliar Roman Canon are few: its title was moved from its position after the Sanctus to the head of the preface dialogue. The priest can choose a preface from a much larger group of options. The words of consecration were revised to match those in the other eucharistic prayers. The memorial acclamation was added. Rubrics were simplified, such as the number of signs of the cross and genuflections. One rubric was moved, probably to create the sense of an epiclesis (more on that below): Formerly the priest extended his hands over the bread and wine during the

Hanc igitur ("Therefore, Lord, we pray"); now he does it during the *Quam oblationem* ("Be pleased, O God, we pray"). The names of many saints were made optional both before and after the consecration. Some sections of the preconciliar Roman Canon concluded with the phrase "Through the same Christ our Lord"; these were shortened to match the phrase that concluded some other sections, "Through Christ our Lord," and all of them were made optional. Although the Consilium considered restructuring the canon more dramatically (for example, joining the prayers for the living and the dead into one section, instead of having them appear in distinct parts of the prayer), its members decided in the interests of antiquity to leave as much intact as possible. Therefore, only these minor changes were made.

Eucharistic Prayer II, however, is another story. It is based on a prayer from the *Apostolic Tradition*, which probably predates the fourth-century Roman Canon. That original prayer first appeared in the *Apostolic Tradition* as a suggestion for a newly ordained bishop who might need help knowing what to say during the Eucharist. The custom at the time called for the presider to improvise the eucharistic prayer,[9] but some bishops were more skilled at this than others. The *Apostolic Tradition*, then, showed its contemporary leaders a model of eucharistic praying. It balanced ownership of the Eucharist between the individual bishop and a recommended order of service.

To prepare the prayer for twentieth-century worshipers, the Consilium's study group on the Order of Mass reworked this early eucharistic prayer so much that it may be regarded as another new composition. Considering the frequency with which presiders choose Eucharistic Prayer II, the success of the work is undisputed. Nonetheless, the results make a case study in how those responsible for the postconciliar Mass exercised ownership over a significant part.

The original eucharistic prayer in the *Apostolic Tradition* contained the same preface dialogue in use today. In fact, this may be the earliest source for the dialogue that starts every eucharistic prayer at every Mass.

Then the original prayer made statements of thanksgiving; for Eucharistic Prayer II these were turned into a preface and given a new introduction based on medieval sources and resembling other prefaces. Originally this section referred to Jesus as a "servant" or a "child," so the study group updated its vocabulary to the more common word "Son." Instead of calling Jesus God's "inseparable word," as the original does, Prayer II simply calls him God's "word"— apparently because of today's more nuanced belief in the persons of the Trinity. The roles of the Holy Spirit and the Virgin Mary were clarified, and the proclamation that Jesus was "manifested" as God's Son at his birth was removed to avoid any inference that he was not God from the moment of his conception. The remainder of Prayer II's preface shortens the original's description of the ministry of Jesus. Furthermore, the priest offering Eucharistic Prayer II may replace its preface with any other one in the Missal's collection. Hence, the entire first part of the prayer as it appeared in the *Apostolic Tradition* may not be heard when Eucharistic Prayer II is offered.

The original prayer had no Sanctus because this acclamation did not enter the Roman Rite until the fifth century. The study group added it so that all the eucharistic prayers would include the same acclamations.

The original prayer proceeded from the words of thanksgiving directly to the institution narrative (the account of the Last Supper), but the study group interposed two brief sections. First it created a bridge to follow the Sanctus, easing the transition to the next part of the prayer. This bridge calls God "the fount of all holiness," an image drawn from a prayer in the Mozarabic Rite, a non-Roman Western liturgical source.[10] As with the collects from the Ambrosian tradition cited above, this supplies another example of how the postconciliar liturgy amplified the sources for the prayers of the Roman Rite.

Second and more importantly, the postconciliar study group moved forward the epiclesis, the petition for the Holy Spirit to change the bread and wine into the Body and Blood of Christ. In the *Apostolic Tradition* the epiclesis held a position later in the eucharistic prayer, but in Eucharistic Prayer II it comes before the institution narrative. No other Eastern or Western eucharistic prayer prior to the Second Vatican Council had put an epiclesis there.

The venerable Roman Canon had no epiclesis. The Roman Rite holds that the consecration of the bread and wine happens at Mass when the priest repeats the words of Jesus from the Last Supper.[11] The eucharistic prayers from Eastern traditions, however, typically include this institution narrative among the reasons why the community has gathered to give God thanks. Eastern anaphoras place the epiclesis after the institution narrative, where, it may be argued, the epiclesis then consecrates. The words of the Roman Canon never explicitly call upon the Holy Spirit to change the elements, a point of much discontent in the East. This explains why the Roman Rite maintains that the institution narrative consecrates, and why the study group moved the extension of the priest's hands over the offering to the *Quam oblationem*, the section of Eucharistic Prayer I that includes the petition, "make it spiritual." The gesture made it appear that an epiclesis is taking place before the institution narrative.

Similar to other anaphoras of the East, the *Apostolic Tradition* has its epiclesis *after* the account of the Last Supper. The very Roman study group revising the prayer was uncomfortable with keeping that sequence because it would then appear that the priest was praying for the Holy Spirit to do something that had already happened. So the group split the final petitions of the *Apostolic Tradition*'s prayer. It placed *before* the institution narrative the petition for the Holy Spirit to come upon the bread and wine, and it left *behind* the petition that the community be united in the Spirit. This split has become the model for all nine of the postconciliar eucharistic prayers of the Roman Rite. Some people have called the second petition an epiclesis over the assembly, but it is not. The only explicit epiclesis in the eucharistic prayers of the Roman Rite is made over the bread and wine; later, the prayer associates the coming of the Holy Spirit into the community with the sacramental communion its members will share, not with any particular moment of the eucharistic prayer.

In composing an epiclesis for Eucharistic Prayer II, the study group chose to include an image from the Gothic Missal: dew.[12] The resultant prayer asks God to send the dew of the Holy Spirit upon the offering.[13] "Dew" is a biblical metaphor for new life, beauty, and nourishment, and it probably seemed like a particularly rich image when the postconciliar group composed its prayer in Latin. Little could they have understood the difficulty of rendering the word in the vernacular languages. The first English translation found the image so unfamiliar that it simply omitted it. The German did the same. The Italian and Spanish translations, by contrast, prayed for the "outpouring" of the Spirit. The French prayed for the "spreading" of the Spirit upon the gifts. None of these major languages translated exactly the word "dew" from the Latin. (This shows one example in which translators exercised ownership of the Mass. More on that below.)

After these transitional elements comes the institution narrative. In revising the one from the *Apostolic Tradition*, the study group expanded it to parallel the content of the narratives in the other eucharistic prayers under development. The group also added the memorial acclamation to achieve the same uniformity.

The *Apostolic Tradition* next wraps the anamnesis together with the offering, a practice that can be traced to West Syrian sources.[14] The anamnesis calls to mind—and affirms present—the death and resurrection of Christ. The offering is the moment that justifies the expression the "sacrifice" of the Mass; it belongs more clearly after the consecration than at the earlier preparation of the gifts, formerly called "the offertory." For this section, the Consilium's study group expanded the vocabulary. The *Apostolic Tradition* referred here to the bread and cup, but the prayer now uses more biblical and theological expressions: "the Bread of life and the Chalice of salvation."

The epiclesis comes next in the *Apostolic Tradition*. Because the postconciliar study group moved it forward for Eucharistic Prayer II, the part left alone echoes the theme of the original: church unity in the Holy Spirit. From there, the *Apostolic Tradition* goes directly to the doxology, but the study group added several parts to its revision: a prayer for the church and its leaders; a prayer for the dead, both Christian and non-Christian; and a prayer that the living may share in eternal life. Similar sections appear in the other postconciliar eucharistic prayers, and even in the Roman Canon, though, unlike Prayer II, their petitions for the living consistently precede their petitions for the dead.

The *Apostolic Tradition*'s doxology is more expanded than the one in use today. The original praises God "in your holy church"—but the study group changed the original doxology to match the one it would use in the other eucharistic prayers.

Eucharistic Prayer II, then, which many believe to be a revived presentation of an ancient prayer, is a prayer highly reworked by the commission Paul VI appointed to prepare the revised liturgy. Although it may appear to be part of a Mass that belongs to the ancients, it belongs to a much later church.

Vernacular Translation

The 1963 Constitution on the Sacred Liturgy permitted an extended use of the vernacular languages, as noted above. The bishops foresaw the importance of proclaiming in the vernacular readings from Scripture and directives addressed to the people, as well as "some of the prayers and chants."[15] Nonetheless, the constitution permitted conferences of bishops to decide on the extent of the vernacular and submit their decrees to the Apostolic See for confirmation.[16] Respecting the vast number of languages spoken by Catholics around the world, the constitution kept the work local: translations "must be approved by the competent territorial ecclesiastical authority,"[17] that is, by the conferences of bishops.

Some argue that the use of the vernacular has gone too far; others, that final approval of translations should be restored to episcopal conferences. It is inadequate to appeal to the council alone for either position. Although the constitution did not directly call for the use of the vernacular throughout the liturgies of the Roman Rite, it laid the path along which this could happen. Although it assigned translation responsibilities to episcopal conferences in 1963, this did not last long.

By 1967, Pope Paul VI invited conferences to submit vernacular translations of the Roman Canon for experimental use.[18] Rather than let them make the final decision on the words, however, Paul asked the conferences to submit their work to his Consilium for confirmation. The Consilium realized that the Roman Canon served as a cornerstone of the Catholic Mass in two respects: it was the most important prayer in the Roman Rite, and it represented only one small entry in the vast collection of prayers and rubrics. The Consilium therefore produced and distributed guidelines for translation in a groundbreaking instruction known by its French title, *Comme le prévoit*.[19]

The Consilium's instruction opens with this key general principle: "it is not sufficient that a liturgical translation merely reproduce the expressions and ideas of the original text. Rather it must faithfully communicate to a given people, and in their own language, that which the Church by means of this given text originally intended to communicate to another people in another time. A faithful translation, therefore, cannot be judged on the basis of individual words: the total context of this specific act of communication must be kept in mind, as well as the literary form proper to the respective language."[20]

Furthermore, *Comme le prévoit* freed translators to reduce the number of adjectives and superlatives in favor of achieving a sense of the whole passage's unit of meaning.[21] It favored the vocabulary in common usage, saying that the words should express "the prayer of some actual community."[22]

With these guidelines, work on the English translation began. A mixed commission of bishops from various conferences took up the task. Near the beginning of the Second Vatican Council, a few bishops from English-speaking countries began dialoguing about a common vernacular translation, partly because "a much higher standard of translation could be achieved through pooling their resources, with the larger countries coming to the aid of smaller and poorer ones."[23] The resulting International Commission on English in the Liturgy (ICEL) held its inaugural meeting at the Venerable English College in Rome on October 17, 1963—two months *before* the council approved the Constitution on the Sacred Liturgy.

ICEL produced an immense body of work in the ensuing years. Consistent with the translation principles then in force, translators chose approachable language aimed at the unit of meaning rather than matched words. The results allowed a generation of English-speaking Catholics to pray the liturgy in their own language for the first time. Many people specifically appreciated the direct approach of the collects; for example, the one for Wednesday of the Third Week of Lent reads: "Lord, during this lenten season nourish us with your word of life and make us one in love and prayer."[24]

ICEL also composed alternative opening prayers for the Sundays and solemnities of the year. Inspired by the original collect, these expressed its sentiments more freely; for example, on the Thirtieth Sunday in Ordinary Time: "Praised be you, God and Father of our Lord Jesus Christ. There is no power for good which does not come from your covenant, and no promise to hope in, that your love has not offered. Strengthen our faith to accept your covenant and give us the love to carry out your command."[25] Many of the prayers were lovely, though some compositional principles could be criticized:

double negatives featured prominently in many of these orations. So did prolixity. So did gender-exclusive language.

Perhaps it was the very publication of the first English translation that raised the issue of gender-inclusive language. The first translators obviously had not seen the problem. For example, the collect for the Third Sunday in Ordinary Time includes the phrase "may bring mankind to unity and peace." The collect the following week has "to love all men as you love them." The alternative opening prayer two weeks later speaks of how God's plan "changed mankind's history." Numberless examples appear throughout the Sacramentary. Many presiders simply edited these words as they recited them, in order to avoid giving offense to women—and men—who increasingly found the vocabulary gender-exclusive and counterproductive for prayer. Some members of the faithful edited the words of the Nicene Creed for the same reason. Instead of saying that Christ came "for us men," some simply said "for us." To some Catholics, gender-inclusive words were a matter of social justice that outweighed the authority of recently printed—yet socially outdated—books.

In time, ICEL continued expanding its library of prayers both translated from the Latin and composed originally in English. ICEL eventually made plans for a second translation of the entire Sacramentary. (More on this below.)

In the end, translators could also claim some ownership of the Mass, as did the priests and people who edited the words they proclaimed.

Conclusions

In the years before and after the Second Vatican Council, the authority for the words and actions of the Catholic Mass was in a variety of hands. It was also clear that the Catholic Mass was not divinely immutable. The church possessed the authority to change its sacred liturgy. In the years after the council, the Mass had a variety of stakeholders:

- The bishops participating in the council approved a constitution authorizing a renewal of the liturgy.

- Pope Paul VI formed a Consilium to implement the vision of the council's bishops.

- The Consilium relied on subgroups of liturgical experts, as well as leaders in specified pastoral settings to experiment with the liturgy while it was under development.

- Worshipers from many centuries past, who left behind a body of liturgical prayers and actions, influenced the preservation of their work and established a template from which new prayers and developments emerged.

- The Congregation for Divine Worship confirmed the work of the Consilium and authorized the publication of revised liturgical rites.

- Translators had freedom to style the vernacular prayers according to the needs of actual congregations.

- Individual priests and people at times made adaptations to the words and actions of the Mass for purposes of clarity, spirituality, or justice.

Whose Mass is it? Ownership of the Mass expanded broadly, partly because of the council's trademark statement that the participation of the people was the aim to be considered above all others.[26] After the council, when the priest faced the people and spoke in the vernacular, using words both ancient and new that had been approved by the highest authorities, Catholics newly felt that the Mass was also theirs.

The Arts

Throughout Christian history, the Mass has inspired the arts. Music, architecture, representational art, and publications have all flourished because of the purpose and needs of the celebration of the Eucharist. In turn, the arts have affected people's expectations of the Mass and its environment. They have shaped spirituality. They also contribute beauty, one of the transcendental properties of being. Beauty inspires love and can naturally lead people to thoughts of God. The arts have always found a happy partnership with worship.

Artists, then, may lay claim to the Catholic Mass.

Music

Gregorian chant was composed exclusively as music for worship. The Constitution on the Sacred Liturgy acknowledged that chant is "specially suited to the Roman liturgy" and "should be given pride of place in liturgical services."[1] The Constitution says that music is a treasure "greater even than that of any other art."[2] When music adorns the words of the Mass, it becomes an extension of the prayers more than any other medium can. When worshipers sing, music is the vehicle that drives their prayer.

Chant developed primarily in monasteries where trained singers led the sacred music on behalf of all those gathered. Most of the chant was too complex for average churchgoers to sing. Still, some simpler chants entered the repertoire of parishes, where even children's choirs could learn them. The dialogues of the Mass used simple chant melodies that adorned sacred conversation with solemnity. Names of the original composers of chant are lost.

As classical music developed, "Mass" became a musical genre like sonatas, symphonies, operas, or oratorios. The Roman Missal supplied the words, and the traditional movements included the Kyrie, Gloria, Credo, Sanctus, Benedictus, and Agnus Dei. The musical setting of a Requiem Mass included additional movements, such as the entrance antiphon (*Requiem*), the sequence (*Dies iræ*), the responsory (*Libera me*), and the antiphon of the absolution (*In paradisum*). Musical styles changed according to the gifts of the composer and the prevailing qualities of great music. Even composers who were not Catholic wrote settings of the Mass.

Among the classics in this genre are the *Missa Papæ Marcelli* by Giovanni Pierluigi da Palestrina (+1594), the *Mass in B Minor* by Johann Sebastian Bach (+1750), the *Requiem Mass in D Minor* by Wolfgang Amadeus Mozart (+1791), the *Missa Brevis in F Major* by Franz Joseph Haydn (+1809), the *Missa Solemnis in D Major* by Ludwig van Beethoven (+1827), the *Requiem* by Giuseppe Verdi (+1901), the *Requiem* by Gabriel Fauré (+1924), and—a popular classic—the *Requiem* by Andrew Lloyd Weber (born 1948).

Some composers have taken freedom with the genre by replacing the traditional movements with other words. Examples include the *German Requiem* of Johannes Brahms (+1897), the *War Requiem* of Benjamin Britten (+1976), and *Mass* by Leonard Bernstein (+1990). When speaking of the world of classical music, to ask "Whose Mass is it?" is to ask the name of the composer, and in some cases, the librettist.

This has changed since the Second Vatican Council. Interest in composing or performing the classical musical genre of a "Mass" has waned. Many reasons can be suggested. For example, even before the council the arts in general were already breaking their strong link to the Catholic Church. The purpose of creating art became more generic, even secular, less Christian, and less Catholic.

Prior to the council, a musical Mass was as much a concert piece as a liturgical one. During a liturgical Mass, the chants were being sung by a choir, not by the congregation. When the Second Vatican Council promoted congregational singing, it changed the perception of the musical genre. This may have had an impact in the broader world of classical music. Many composers wrote settings of the Mass to be sung during the liturgy, but newly composed concert music utilizing the movements of the Mass has virtually disappeared.

The Electric Prunes had released a *Mass in F Minor* in 1968, a studio recording of the traditional movements of a Mass sung in Latin and Greek. David Brubeck (+2012) composed a setting of the postconciliar texts at the request of *Our Sunday Visitor*. The resulting *Mass to Hope* included a setting of one of the eucharistic prayers for Masses of reconciliation. The score envisions choirs, soloists, jazz musicians, and orchestra. Yet Brubeck conceived it as a piece of liturgical music, not specifically for the concert hall.

By the time of the council, jazz, rock, and country had taken hold of popular music. Yet the style that most influenced the composition of postconciliar music was folk. Surely the desire for music that congregations could sing caused this to happen. Even today, the main producers of Catholic liturgical music in the United States (GIA Publications, Oregon Catholic Press, and World Library Publications) provide a repertoire that is melodically and rhythmically safe. Some music composed for young Catholics uses rock rhythms, but it is hard for any congregation to sing correctly. At times a congregation will simplify the rhythms and the melody into something they can sing. Folk music, for better or worse, is more practical for the full, conscious, active participation of the people.

Although the three main publishers dominate the market in the United States, some local musicians compose unpublished music for use in their own parishes, monasteries, and convents. Whereas this gives local musicians a platform to test their skills, it may be diminishing their community's ability to learn repertoire they will need in common celebrations outside their own parish church or monastic enclosure.

The United States Conference of Catholic Bishops does not authorize publication of music that makes alteration to the official texts of the Mass. For example, a setting of the Lamb of God for Marty Haugen's *Mass of Creation* used to contain the words, "Jesus, Lamb of God, you take away the sins of the world." The word "Jesus" is not in the Missal, however, so the composer rewrote the phrase without that word, in order to comply with the conference's preferences.[3]

The same restrictions do not apply to some other language groups. Many settings composed for the Mass in Spanish, for example, take great freedom with the words as they appear in the Missal. Some composers have even altered the words of the Lord's Prayer to accommodate a musical style or evoke a spiritual emotion. In Germany, the national hymnal *Gotteslob* contains a whole section of music that can be sung in place of the Gloria. Nearly all of settings are either paraphrases or hymns bearing some thematic link to it.[4] In those cultures, then, some of the very words of the Order of Mass are in the hands of composers and lyricists.

Congregational singing has become a powerful component of the Catholic experience of the Mass. A few Catholics prefer no music at all, and some parishes offer a quiet Sunday Mass with no singing, but these are by far the exception. If congregational singing is not being offered, people sense that something is wrong.

At funerals, the classic requiem chants are rarely performed, but a small body of popular music has nearly replaced them.[5] Priests or parish funeral coordinators commonly ask the family for musical suggestions, and the family will commonly share what they have experienced at other funerals. This keeps the repertoire small, but it does promote singing.

The amount of liturgical music published in English has reached explosive proportions. The high demand for congregational singing met the competitive instincts of publishing houses. This volume of new music came at the expense of the traditional entrance, offertory, and communion chants of the Mass. Prior to the council, the words of these chants were fixed irreplaceably. Each Sunday could be identified by the opening words of its *introit*. This is how Sundays got named *Gaudete*, *Lætare*, and *Quasimodo*. This is also the source for calling a funeral a *Requiem* Mass; that is the first word of the entrance chant.

The postconciliar General Instruction of the Roman Missal (GIRM) permits these antiphons to be replaced, however, with "another liturgical chant that is suited to the sacred action, the day, or the time of year."[6] That permission, repeated for the communion chant,[7] caused a large-scale abandonment of the antiphons fixed for each Mass. The offertory chant, which still exists in lesser known liturgical books such as the *Graduale Romanum*, is not mentioned in the GIRM, nor does the text for this traditional antiphon appear anywhere in the Missal. Consequently, it is nearly universally replaced with other music or with silence.

When planners are asked to explain how they choose the music for the entrance chant, they usually say that they follow themes from the gospel or the lectionary's other readings of the day. There is virtually no liturgical tradition behind such a choice, nor was the lectionary compiled to influence music outside the Liturgy of the Word. On occasion, one finds a link between the words of the Missal's communion chant and the gospel of the day. But planners often choose the music for communion because the words contain some reference to the Body and Blood of Christ, a custom quite rare in the Missal. The Missal's communion chants have their own inner logic. Some have been associated with specific days at least since the eighth century, such as the one for the First Sunday of Advent. Others form an inner group, such as the "I am" statements of Jesus in John's gospel, which appear on the Third, Twelfth, Eighteenth, Twentieth, Twenty-Third, and Twenty-Fifth Sundays in Ordinary Time. Verses from the Beatitudes appear on the Fourth, Fifth, Seventeenth, and Twenty-Second Sundays in Ordinary Time. The words of these particular communion chants were new to the postconciliar Mass, and they invited a unique way of planning music. But these internal structures are commonly set aside when planners choose music that focuses more on the action of going to Communion.

Thus, once the GIRM untethered the entrance and communion music from the texts in the Missal, the ownership of the music—and of some of the central texts of the Catholic Mass—went into the hands of parish musicians. Normally the choice seems oblivious to the text that the Missal proposes for the day. The freedom to choose alternative words and the attractively complex texture of the lectionary have exercised a profound influence on the musical choices of the Mass for the first time in history.

In the past, the music for Mass was fairly limited. The Gregorian chants appointed for each day could be heard in communities with the skills to perform them. Many of the greatest composers of Western music history included a Mass among their works—even if they were not Catholic. Today's classical composers do not so strongly sense the same urge. The music for Mass has moved from the concert hall to the church, and the song has moved from the choirs to the congregations. This has changed the style of music performed in church, as well as the place of authority. Because musical choices are in the hands of people at each parish, it has increased the local musician's sense of ownership in the Mass.

Architecture

Prior to the council, the basilica provided the basic model for the design of a Catholic church. The building was rectangular, often with an apse at one narrow end, which framed the sanctuary inside. People entered the church through doors at the opposite end and occupied pews facing the sanctuary. The height of the building created a sense of majesty and awe.

Originally, basilicas were not churches. In first-century Rome, basilicas served as practical public meeting spaces. The ones constructed for the Roman Forum helped people gather in numbers for some purpose (a speech or a meeting, for example.) Those in charge of the assembly could stand in the apse to be heard. Windows pierced the upper reaches of the two long walls. Thus, the shape of the building provided acoustics, light, and a practical arrangement for dealing with a number of people enclosed in one space.

As Christianity began to flourish, the celebration of the Eucharist moved from people's homes to designated public spaces. To develop its own buildings in these early centuries, the church turned to basilicas for inspiration. Structurally sound and practically fit, basilicas provided an appropriate place for large numbers of Christians to gather. In time, the buildings' floor plan had an impact on the liturgy—distinguishing on one axis the areas occupied by the ministers and by the congregation, and creating on the other axis an aisle for processions.

In recent centuries, the invention of electricity allowed more diversity to the classic design. Electrical lights diminished the need for clerestory windows, and electrical sound reinforcement diminished the acoustical reliance on the shape of the building.

After the Second Vatican Council, other factors had an immediate impact on church design. Most importantly, the council called for the full, conscious, active participation of the people: "And when churches are to be built, let great care be taken that they be suitable for the celebration of liturgical services and for the active participation of the faithful."[8]

Long, narrow naves would no longer be conducive to participation at a Catholic Mass. They served well when the liturgical activity of ministers in the sanctuary tolerated some distance from the devotional exercises of the people in the pews. But now that the faithful were to respond in dialogue with the priest and deacon, to watch and hear and pray together as one, pews placed at a distance from the sanctuary were frustrating the design of the liturgical reform.

Consequently, many postconciliar Catholic church buildings were designed in the shape of a fan. In this way, without altering the size of the sanctuary, the nave spread wider, allowing more people proximity to the primary liturgical action with which they were expected to engage.

Furthermore, when the Vatican permitted the priest to stand behind a freestanding altar, this immediately changed the appearance of the sanctuary. In the past, the altar faced the back wall of the church and a tabernacle sat upon the altar. Now the tabernacle must be located in a place apart from the main altar.[9] Some Catholics colloquially refer to the entire sanctuary as "the altar"; the confusion was more understandable in the preconciliar design.

With a wider building and an altar resembling a freestanding table, with a priest poised behind the altar to engage the people more naturally in dialogues, the faithful increased their participation at the Mass.

The nave also took on a different purpose. In the past it was an area that fostered private devotion. Statues, candles, and Stations of the Cross—all objects of personal devotion—helped the faithful focus during the Mass when they were not actively participating in the sacred action in the sanctuary. Now that they were beginning to participate differently, the preferred location of these objects of personal devotion shifted. Repositioning devotional objects to subsidiary places in new and renovated churches streamlined the nave. The faithful could more easily focus on the activity in the sanctuary and join in the common prayer.

The location of the tabernacle became a source of much contention. Because Catholics were being encouraged to participate at the common celebration and to share Communion from the bread and wine consecrated on the altar,[10] the purpose of the tabernacle had come into sharper focus: It housed the extra consecrated bread for the purposes of bringing Communion to the sick. It provided a source for extra communion breads if ministers ran short during the distribution of Communion at Mass. It became an object of devotion for the people.

And not just any object of devotion: The tabernacle, because it houses the Blessed Sacrament, is the most sacred object in any Catholic church building. This led many people to conclude that it belonged in the most central place in the building. Churches are designed for the celebration of the Eucharist, however, not for adoration of the Blessed Sacrament in the tabernacle. Consequently, many parish leaders moved the tabernacle to side altars in their sanctuaries. These had first been constructed so that more than one priest could celebrate Mass at the same time, but the postconciliar permission for concelebration had virtually eliminated their purpose. Since the tabernacle had rested on the high altar in the past, some simply moved it to a secondary altar in a renovated church. Some new church buildings created Blessed Sacrament chapels especially to house the tabernacle. The displacement of the tabernacle from center to side emphasized the centrality of the altar, "the center toward which the attention of the whole congregation of the faithful naturally turns."[11] These design changes were meant to foster the participation of the people during Mass, but some people misread it as an insult to God and a lack of belief in the real presence of Christ in the Blessed Sacrament.

Complicating the message, many priests continued to use the tabernacle, no matter where it was located, for the distribution of Communion to the faithful at every Mass. It seemed odd to some people that the central object of their devotion, from which they regularly received sacramental Communion, was kept to the side. Their connection to Communion from the altar was never firmly established. The practice of distributing Communion from the tabernacle implies a clericalism that the priest receives from the altar at every Mass, but some laity receive from the previously consecrated breads in the tabernacle at every Mass.

The decision on tabernacle *placement* now falls to the bishop because of legislation that is new to the third edition of the Roman Missal.[12]

Nevertheless, priests exercise nearly absolute control over the *usage* of the tabernacle during the distribution of Communion. (More on this below.)

Baptismal fonts often have a new location in postconciliar church design. Formerly, the fonts usually stood inside small rooms or chapels suitable for the gathering of the priest, parents, and god-parents. The revised Rite of Baptism for Children presumes, however, that the baptistery should be large enough to accommodate a congregation.[13] If it is not, the sacrament may be celebrated at a suitable place within the church where all can take part.

In many postconciliar churches the font stands prominently in the nave. A font may be near the front door, for example, where the faithful may use it as the holy water stoup upon entering the building and from which holy water may be drawn for the opening of a funeral Mass. This helps people renew their baptismal commitment every time they use holy water. The participation of the people at baptisms has caused the redesign of church baptismal fonts.

Confessionals too have been redesigned and repositioned. Formerly, confessionals commonly occupied space within the nave, the very place where private devotions flowered and where a private confession seemed to fit. Now, however, a priest is not to hear confessions in a church while another priest is celebrating Mass.[14] Consequently, some churches have located the confessionals in other areas—near the gathering space or in private chapels. In this way, the purpose of the nave is kept clear for the whole assembly to celebrate the Eucharist.

These factors have affected the outside appearance of postconciliar churches as well. With buildings of greater width and the use of electrical lighting, height became secondary. With electrical sound reinforcement, the functional need for an apse disappeared. Consequently, the exterior of postconciliar church buildings does not always resemble the basilican style. Some people prefer "a church that looks like a church"—meaning a towering basilica with stained-glass windows. The participation of the people, however, has changed the floor plan, which logically influenced changes to the exterior. The result should enhance participation, and that will redefine what makes a church look like a church.

Architects, then, have considerable influence over how the Mass is celebrated. The shape of churches determines the length of processions, the ease of participation, the sound of music, and the visibility so necessary for people to feel a part of the action. Conferences of bishops and individual dioceses have issued guidelines for church buildings. But many decisions happen on a local level with parish building committees. Members will make better choices if they have learned about the purpose of Catholic church buildings, and they will have considerable influence over how people experience the Mass in their local parish church.

Art

Many Catholic churchgoers establish deep spiritual attachments to visual works of art. Almost every church has a crucifix, statues, or other images that help Catholics connect more strongly to their faith. Most visual art is designed for private veneration rather than for the liturgy. Although statues and paintings are peripheral to the celebration of the Eucharist, many Catholics move seamlessly between the ritual of the Mass and the devotional images that adorn it. Both occupy the same building.

Catholic piety is incarnational in the sense that it discerns spiritual meaning inside natural elements. Christians believe that the Word of God became flesh, uniting the uncreated and created worlds. Catholics use bread and wine, oil and water, palm branches and ashes, candles and cloths to experience God's presence. The sound of the human voice and the wooden pipes of an organ all keep Catholics close to nature, where they encounter its Creator.

Visual art often relies on the natural world for inspiration, and through it Catholics can reaffirm their beliefs. They meditate on scenes from the Bible in general and the life of Christ in particular, especially the stations of his passion. They pray before images of saints long dead. They pour out their hearts before the unpredictable yet comforting flicker of a candle set before a religious image.

Some of the most exquisite works of art in the world were created for Catholic church buildings—Michelangelo's *Pietá*, Caravaggio's *Deposition of Christ from the Cross*, the stained glass inside the Sainte-Chapelle in Paris, and *Christ on the Cross* by Diego Velázquez. Stunning as they are, they have set an impossibly high standard. Works of lesser beauty adorn nearly every church, yet they still have power to stir a believer's heart. If someone walks into a church and moves a statue, hides a crucifix, or obstructs a painting, even with the intent of making the space more liturgical, the act may disrupt someone else's spiritual well-being. Consequently, those who manage the creation and placement of art have an impact on the believer's total experience of the Catholic Mass.

After the Second Vatican Council, the traditional media for church art perdured: statues, paintings, tapestries, and stained glass, for example. Some additional media developed: banners, for example, because, like folk music, almost every parish had someone who could produce them. Fashioned from inexpensive felt, they required the common tools of scissors, paste, and imagination. Even people without much artistic skill could make banners. Some people, awakened to the invitation to participate at Mass, thus contributed to the environment of the celebration. Proclaiming words and posting symbols, banners spoke immediately to worshipers. Vestments also became a medium for conveying messages of celebration. Like banners, many chasubles and stoles were made by local artisans. As with music, the style of art shifted from classical to folk, riding the populist wave of participation.

As mentioned above, the preferred location for devotional images began to move from the sanctuary and the nave into more secluded areas. Statues played a dominant role in people's experience of the preconciliar Mass because they provided points of meditation for those not absorbed in the intricacies of the ritual. Now the faithful are encouraged to participate completely in the Mass, and some images have been moved to create separate spaces for private devotion and to free the space where the community focuses on common liturgical action.

Related to this artistic trend was ecumenical sensitivity. Many other Christians do not share Catholics' devotion to the saints. They have little tradition of praying to saints, so they keep images of them spare. Those who revised the postconciliar general calendar for the Catholic liturgical year removed quite a few saints who were popular only in some regions, or whose biographies were historically questionable. Most famously, St. Christopher left the general calendar because of insufficiently reliable biographical evidence pertaining to him. Nonetheless, sales of his medals continue apace because many Catholics make few distinctions between popular devotion and official liturgy. The decision to make optional the names of most of the saints in the

Roman Canon is another example where ecumenical sensitivity may have influenced the Roman liturgy. Eucharistic Prayer III allowed for the inclusion of the name of the saint of the day or the local patron, but Prayers II and IV did not. Even in Prayer III, the saint is listed not as an intercessor but as one in whose company the community hopes to share. Other Christians who may object to the intercession of saints would more easily pray to enjoy their company. The name of Jesus' mother, Mary, remained in each of the prayers, but the number of other saints called by name was greatly reduced. Catholics can pray a eucharistic prayer without cataloguing lists of saints. This ecumenical sensitivity to the liturgy fostered Christian unity and built trust. (More on this later.)

It was surprising, then, in 2013, when the Vatican authorized the inclusion of the name of Saint Joseph in Prayers II, III, and IV. (Joseph was already mentioned in Prayer I.) Most Catholics responded quite favorably to the change; however, it overlooked the ecumenical thrust of this aspect of these eucharistic prayers. The church was trying not to curtail devotion to the saints but to keep it from affecting liturgical goals. The earliest extant eucharistic prayers made no mention of saints. For ecumenical sensitivity, historical accuracy, and theological integrity, the postconciliar eucharistic prayers kept the role of the saints at a minimum.

The simplification of statues and images followed suit. The official guideline suggests only one image per saint per sanctuary: "Care should, therefore, be taken that their number not be increased indiscriminately, and moreover that they be arranged in proper order so as not to draw the attention of the faithful to themselves and away from the celebration itself."[15]

Through the various modes of art, those who had a say in how Catholics experienced the Mass included pastors and patrons, artisans and artists, musicians and theologians. Efforts were made to maximize people's participation in the liturgy through the making of art and placing it judiciously on the church grounds.

Publications

The principal books for the Catholic Mass are the Missal and the Lectionary. Auxiliary materials include participation aids for the people.

Prior to the council, the Lectionary and the Missal shared the same book. When they separated, the Lectionary became a multivolume work, leaving behind a book called *Missale Romanum* in Latin but which was called *The Sacramentary* in the United States. Without the readings, this book partly resembled medieval sacramentaries. Because of the long tradition that the readings appeared in the Missal, the title page inside the Lectionary still calls it "The Roman Missal: The Lectionary." The "missal," then, is a library of books used for the Catholic Mass. When the Sacramentary underwent a revised translation, its name changed to the Roman Missal, but that is only one volume of many.

Participation aids for the faithful proliferated. Many worshipers appreciate having something in their hands to help them pray along. At a minimum, if they are expected to sing, they need words and preferably notes. Many, though, want more than music.

Commonly the daily Scripture readings from the Lectionary appear in worship aids for the people. This has tempted some lectors to proclaim the readings at Mass from convenient leaflets instead of the official liturgical book. People unfamiliar with the structure of the Lectionary and the affect of the liturgical calendar may have trouble locating the readings of the day. For them, it is easier to use a seasonal, disposable publication. But the General Introduction to the Lectionary says, "Because of the dignity of the Word of God, the books of readings used in the celebration are not to be replaced by other pastoral aids, for example, by leaflets printed for the preparation of the readings by the faithful or for their personal meditation."[16]

Several times the GIRM reminds the faithful that they are to listen to the readings.[17] Nevertheless, many read along privately instead of giving full attention with their ears. If the parish does not supply copies of the readings, people have other means of obtaining them. They may subscribe to a periodical or use an app on a smartphone. They should be listening instead, but their behavior is nearly impossible to control. Some argue that they cannot hear the readings well due to poor amplification or ill-prepared readers. Yet these problems can be mitigated if people prepare for Mass by praying over the readings at home.

The Catholic Church is somewhat unique in its request that people participate in the Liturgy of the Word by listening rather than reading. Some other Christian churches encourage members to bring a

Bible to church and to follow along with the proclamations and preaching. But the GIRM explains the Catholic position: "When the Sacred Scriptures are read in the Church, God himself speaks to his people, and Christ, present in his word, proclaims the Gospel."[18] Nonetheless, many people take control of the Liturgy of the Word, putting publications they have purchased into the service of the liturgy.

The main books, the Missal and the Lectionary, are published in substantial volumes to signify the dignity and beauty of their contents. This is even more true of the Book of the Gospels, which often bears ornate decoration. The GIRM supports the idea: "Special care must be taken to ensure that the liturgical books, particularly the Book of the Gospels and the Lectionary, which are intended for the proclamation of the Word of God and hence receive special veneration, are to be in a liturgical action truly signs and symbols of higher realities and hence should be truly worthy, dignified, and beautiful."[19]

To prepare for the revised English translation of the Missal in 2011, the United States Conference of Catholic Bishops allowed seven publishers to produce the book. This contrasted with most other English-speaking episcopal conferences, which contracted with a single publisher. Publishers followed common guidelines, but they received sufficient freedom in areas such as paper, binding, artwork, ribbons, pagination, and fonts.

Publishers exercise more freedom in producing participation aids. They determine the repertoire of music. They may promote specific liturgical options in cases where a larger variety is available. For example, on All Souls Day, the parish may choose from dozens of Scripture passages among the Lectionary's Masses for the dead. Participation aids acknowledge this, but they usually print a specific selection of the publisher's own choosing. Homilists are free to preach on other readings, but readers who are unaware of the options available may assume that the correct readings are the ones in the leaflet, not in the Lectionary. Publishers, then, also have a voice in how the Mass is celebrated.

Electronic publication has dramatically changed the history of books. This evolution probably marks the most pivotal publishing innovation since Gutenberg's movable type. Printed materials are less universal; many people use an electronic device to read journals and books, or to participate at Mass. Some priests use one too. They can find the sacred texts and select a larger font on a device more lightweight than the third edition of the Missal.

Nevertheless, Church authorities frown on the practice. The New Zealand Catholic Bishops Conference expressly forbade priests to use electronic applications at Mass. They praise the excellence of such apps for study purposes, but "only the official printed copy of the Roman Missal may be used at Mass and at the Church's other liturgies."[20] The bishops reason that the Catholic Church, like other faiths, has "sacred books which are reserved for those rituals and activities which are at the heart of the faith."[21] The physical book is an incarnational sign of God's word and the church's prayer.

Objectors face the inexorable march of history. The Liturgy of the Hours was revised after the council to provide a liturgical prayer book any Catholic could follow. The vagaries of the liturgical year, however, necessitated a complicated layout in an expensive, four-volume work, and many people found it too difficult to master, too cumbersome for prayer. On an app, though, the hours are simpler to pray. The app has already sorted through the texts necessary for the day. Not all the options are available; like publishers, developers exercise their discretion. But the Liturgy of the Hours, which began its life on parchments calligraphed by monks, has newfound popularity because of apps developed by engineers.

Some religious goods stores market a stand suitable for holding an electronic reader or tablet. It rests easily on a table—or on an altar. But church authorities do not promote it because of the tradition behind the sacrality of books.

Among those with a voice in the postconciliar church are publishers of liturgical books and participation aids. They have designed the sacred books put to use during the Mass, as well as the booklets and apps that many people keep close at hand in order to help them pray. The Mass belongs to publishers too.

Conclusions

The arts have continued to make a profound impact on the way that Catholics pray as a body and as individuals. The postconciliar outreach to the arts reached a certain populist level because of the desire for the active participation of the people. The question, "Whose Mass is it?" receives a diverse answer in this field.

- Composers provide music for people to sing, music that will touch the soul and help people experience the emotional complexities of their faith.
- Parish musicians make choices that color the prayers and creeds that people hear and sing.
- Architects shape buildings to encourage the participation of people.
- Artists provide visible ways to connect with people's faith in invisible realities.
- Publishers produce books and other media that lend dignity to the celebration and ease for participation.

The Catholic Church continues to provide a home for the arts. When they achieve beauty, they lift the soul that seeks out God.

Variations

The changes to the Mass after the Second Vatican Council affected a variety of groups both inside and outside Roman Catholicism. Within the Roman communion, some groups wanted further adaptations to the rites. Those outside paid attention to the Roman developments because they caused further reflection on their own approaches to Sunday worship. Even those outside Catholicism felt some ownership of the Catholic Mass.

"An Order of the Mass for India"

The Constitution on the Sacred Liturgy had authorized regional adaptations,[1] so the Catholic Bishops' Conference of India proposed twelve points, all of which the Cardinal President of the Consilium, Benno Gut, accepted in 1969. The list follows:

1. The posture during Mass, both for the priests and the faithful, may be adapted to the local usage, that is, sitting on the floor,[2] standing, and the like; footwear may be removed also.

2. Genuflections may be replaced by the profound bow with the *anjali hasta*.[3]

3. A *panchanga pranam*[4] by both priests and faithful can take place before the liturgy of the word, as part of the penitential rite, and at the conclusion of the anaphora.

4. Kissing of objects may be adapted to local custom, that is touching the object with one's fingers or palm of one's hand and bringing the hands to one's eyes or forehead.

5. The kiss of peace could be given by the exchange of the *anjali hasta* and/or the placing of the hands of the giver between the hands of the recipient.

6. Incense could be made more use of in liturgical services. The receptacle could be the simple incense bowl with handle.

7. The vestments could be simplified. A single tunic-type chasuble with a stole (*angavastra*)[5] could replace the traditional vestments of the Roman Rite. Samples of this change are to be forwarded to the Consilium.

8. The corporal could be replaced by a tray (*thali* or *thambola thattu*) of fitting material.

9. Oil lamps could be used instead of candles.

10. The preparatory rite of the Mass may include:
    a. the presentation of gifts;
    b. the welcome of the celebrant in an Indian way, e.g., with a single *arati*,[6] washing of hands, etc.;
    c. the lighting of the lamp;
    d. the greetings of peace among the faithful in sign of mutual reconciliation.

11. In the *Oratio fidelium*[7] some spontaneity may be permitted both with regard to its structure and the formulation of the intentions. The universal aspect of the Church, however, should not be left in oblivion.

12. In the offertory rite, and at the conclusion of the anaphora, the Indian form of worship may be integrated, that is, double or triple *arati* of flowers, and/or incense, and/or light.[8]

These points were printed in the 1986 Indian edition of the Roman Missal, and local bishops had authority to put them into place as much or little as they saw fit.

The Consilium had also said that a new Indian anaphora would be "most welcomed."[9] This flowed from an article in the Constitution on the Sacred Liturgy that indicated, "Even in the liturgy the Church has no wish to impose a rigid uniformity in matters that do not affect the faith or the good of the whole community."[10] A draft of an Indian eucharistic prayer was presented at the Third All India Liturgical Meeting in 1971. By that time, however, the Congregation for Divine Worship said that all earlier permissions for experimentation with the Mass "are to be considered as no longer in effect."[11] Nonetheless, the National Biblical Catechetical and Liturgical Centre in Bangalore published an experimental new order for the Mass, which included the optional proclamation of Indian scriptures in addition to the biblical readings, and the proposed Indian anaphora.[12] This Order of Mass was designed for private circulation and experimentation. The following year the Congregation for Divine Worship explicitly stopped the use of the Indian anaphora, but other adaptations continued to be used at Bangalore.

Some people called it an Indian Rite Mass, but no such title was ever sought or approved. The adaptations did not attempt to form an Indian Rite but to inculturate the Roman Rite. According to an instruction by the Congregation for Divine Worship and the Discipline of the Sacraments (CDWDS), "inculturation responds to the needs of a particular culture and leads to adaptations which still remain part of the Roman rite."[13] Pope John Paul II saw the same reality through a different lens when he said that inculturation "is a question of collaborating so that the Roman rite, maintaining its own identity, may incorporate suitable adaptations."[14]

The new adaptations promoted by the National Biblical Catechetical and Liturgical Centre provoked so much controversy that the original, approved twelve points for inculturation came back under scrutiny. One problem is that they were based on customs in high-caste Brahminic Hinduism, whereas the majority of Christians in India come from different cultural backgrounds: Dravidian, tribal, and so forth.

It is largely considered that the twelve points remain in force, to the extent that the local bishop permits. But it has been unclear whether these points introduced adaptations that replaced elements of the Roman Order of Mass or if they were to be added in.

Some of the twelve points have been in use in parts of India for many years. The Catholic Bishops' Conference of India has not taken a vote to stop celebration of the national Centre's more broadly adapted Mass, but its usage has diminished along with its support. Even so, the saga demonstrates that ownership of the Roman Mass appeals to non-Roman cultures.

Zaire Usage

Known today as the Democratic Republic of the Congo, the Republic of Zaire was the name of this central African nation from 1971 to 1997. It had been called the Belgian Congo prior to independence in 1960, then the Republic of the Congo (1960–1964), and also the Democratic Republic of the Congo (1964–1971). Its first years of independence coincided with the opening of the Second Vatican Council. Even before the council, local bishops had appealed to Rome for an adapted liturgy for Africa, and they received authorization in 1970. After years of experimentation and approval, the *Missel romain pour les diocèses du Zaïre* was published in 1988. Although the name of the country has since changed, the inculturation of the liturgy is commonly called the Zaire Usage.[15] It is "the only complete non-experimental incultur-ated eucharistic celebration approved after Vatican II."[16]

The Congregation for Divine Worship insisted that the Order of Mass from the Roman Rite serve as the starting point for the inculturation. In the early work, the version was being called the "Zairean Rite," but this was changed to "Zaire Usage" largely because the results are seen as an expression of the Roman Rite. It exists in forms both solemn and simple. The remarks that follow pertain to the solemn form.[17]

The clergy may wear vestments of the vibrant colors typical to the region. Musicians may employ indigenous instruments. All participants—ministers and the faithful—may dance in procession or in their places.

Added to the liturgical ministers is the announcer, a role borrowed from typical African assemblies. The announcer acts as a kind of emcee, explaining the purpose of the celebration and its parts, introducing the various ministers as they take their roles, and animating the people's participation. A layman or laywoman may serve as the announcer.

The faithful bring some offering to the Eucharist—not just bread and wine, but other gifts for the poor or the community. The announcer opens the liturgy by sounding a bell or a gong and calling everyone to silence. Ministers enter carrying a symbol of their ministry. All sing and dance the opening song. The ministers in the procession form a semicircle around the altar, while the presider raises his arms in the form of a V and lowers his head to each side of the altar in turn.

The liturgy opens not with the penitential act but with an invocation of ancestors. Imitating a custom common to other African assemblies, nothing further happens until the deceased are invoked. They once served as models for the community and now act as intercessors. Although their names are not spoken aloud, they are remembered through the lighting of incense and more song and dance. This reverence to the ancestors is similar but not identical to the Catholic devotion to the saints. Ancestors are remembered locally, not through a formal canonization process.

After the Gloria and the opening prayer, all sit. Each lector asks a blessing from the presider. This imitates a practice that some people carry out before tribal chiefs at public assemblies. The announcer introduces the readings. All stand for the enthronement of the gospel, but they sit for its proclamation. In many parts of Africa, sitting—not standing—shows respect. The Roman custom of sitting for the first readings and standing for the gospel diminishes its proclamation to many Africans. The homily may take the form of a dialogue and may be embellished by songs and dances.

The penitential rite is moved to this position after the homily. In some African cultures, forgiveness is sought after circumstances of disharmony are exposed.[18] The homily serves as an opportunity for people to ponder what needs healing, and it opens the way to the penitential act. Participants cross their arms in the form of an X during the penitential rite.

From this expression of sorrow flows the sign of peace. Participants may wash their hand in a common bowl, and then use both hands to greet their neighbors. Holy water may be sprinkled. The prayer of the faithful concludes this part of the liturgy, bringing to God the desire for peace and reconciliation among peoples and with all creation.

Those who bring the eucharistic gifts in procession dance along the way. All others may join the dance from their places in the assembly.

A gong sounds before the eucharistic prayer so that the announcer may deliver an introduction. The anaphora is an adaptation of Eucharistic Prayer II of the Roman Rite. Many of the presidential prayers have been adapted to express a more African worldview through prose and imagery. The people interject acclamations through the final part of the eucharistic prayer, calling out, "Lord, remember them all." The conclusion of the prayer is not just a single amen; the people embellish the final line of the prayer with acclamations, raising their hands in praise.

The communion and closing rites are nearly identical to those of the Roman Order of Mass. Although the Zaire Usage is only one expression of the Roman Rite, its inculturation shows that the Mass belongs to diverse peoples outside the ambit of Europe.

Aboriginal Inculturation

Efforts at evangelization in Australia have successfully reached Aboriginal people, with whom—and in honor of whom—some liturgical inculturation has taken place. The Australian circumstances differ slightly from those in New Zealand, where one Aboriginal culture, the Māori, dominates. The revised English translation of the Roman Missal for Aotearoa New Zealand includes an Order of Mass in two local languages: English and Māori sit side by side on the pages. The New Zealand missal primarily presents a translation, not a liturgical adaptation, although some inculturation is practiced. Australia, however, is home to many different Aboriginal peoples, and liturgical expression has moved beyond translation into inculturation.

The most significant early celebration of an inculturated Mass took place during the Melbourne Eucharistic Congress in 1973.[19] The liturgy unfolded at the Sidney Myer Music Bowl, where thirty thousand people participated at the Mass—far more than could fit in the renovated St. Patrick's Cathedral. In the first years of the liturgical renewal, eucharistic congresses at Bombay (1965) and Bogotá (1968) had caught the fervor of renewed Catholic prayer. In Melbourne a series of liturgical events was prepared for the week-long congress: "Combined migrants' liturgy," "A meeting of the people of God," "A liturgy for children," "Liturgy for senior citizens, sick and handicapped," "A liturgy for youth," "Australian Aboriginal Liturgy," "Pontifical

Divine Liturgy in the Byzantine Rite," and a *"Statio Orbis,"*[20] in which congregations around the world celebrated the liturgy simultaneously with the Mass in Melbourne. All liturgical preparations were made by the Melbourne diocesan liturgical commission in conjunction with the Congregation for Divine Worship. Melbourne's archbishop, James Knox, would become the cardinal prefect of that congregation the following year.

Bishops, missionary priests, and sisters of the Northern Territories and Western Australia contributed to the work on the Australian Aboriginal Liturgy. Hilton Deakin, a Melbourne priest and an anthropologist, coordinated the efforts with the support of Archbishop Knox. Deakin later formed the Aboriginal Catholic Ministry (1991) and became an auxiliary bishop of Melbourne in 1993. The papal legate, Cardinal Lawrence Shehan, presided.

The congress Aboriginal liturgy included additional songs and refrains to be sung by the congregation. The only reading was a proclamation of the gospel account of the Last Supper. A group of twenty-four Tiwi people from Bathurst Island, Northern Territories, mimed the story during its proclamation, in keeping with Aboriginal traditions that promote telling stories with both words and gestures. This proclamation also included song and dance.

In place of the responsorial psalm, a representative from Port Keats sang praise to Christ in the local dialect, accompanied by didgeridoo, clapping sticks, and guitar.[21]

Most importantly, a new eucharistic prayer was composed, and the Vatican approved its usage. It included acclamations during the preface, such as "Heavenly Father!" and "Father, you are good!" The Sanctus was completely reworked, eliminating the threefold "Holy" at the beginning and the Aramaic word "Hosanna." The acclamatory style is evident: "Father, you are good. We are happy about that man Jesus, your only proper Son. Father, you are good. Come, Lord Jesus, come and be with us!"[22] More acclamations by the people during the rest of the prayer sustained a dialogic style. Artisans from the Pallotine Mission station near Broome made the chalice, shaped like the common vessel called a coolamon.[23]

An antiphon preceded and followed the Lord's Prayer: "You are our Father; you live in heaven. We talk to you. Father, you are good."[24] After Communion the period of thanksgiving was expressed in dance.

The Vatican's support for these developments at the congress prompted the continued use of some elements in some parts of Australia. For example, the eucharistic prayer was approved for the Dioceses of Darwin (Northern Territories) and Broome (Western Australia).[25] In 1986 Pope John Paul II visited Alice Springs in the Diocese of Darwin. Speaking to Australia's indigenous people, he said, "The gospel of Our Lord Jesus Christ speaks all languages. It esteems and embraces all cultures. All over the world people worship God and read his word in their own language, and colour the great signs and symbols of religion with touches of their own traditions. Why should you be different from them in this regard, why should you not be allowed the happiness of being with God and each other in Aboriginal fashion? Seek out the best things of your traditional ways. The Church herself in Australia will not be fully the Church that Jesus wants her to be until you have made your contribution to her life and until that contribution has been joyfully received by others."[26]

The National Aboriginal and Torres Strait Islander Catholic Council (NATSICC) produces a kit each year to help with the observance of NATSICC Day in early July. The kit supplies ideas for liturgical inculturation. For example, in 2003 a suggestion appeared for the penitential rite: "A Rite of Water Blessing: It is customary in some areas, when Aboriginal people gather for important ceremonies to use water. Water containers can be a large shell or coolamon and a small branch from an appropriate native tree can be used to sprinkle the water. Please collaborate with your local Indigenous group to ensure this rite of water blessing is appropriate."[27]

Other ideas continue to appear.[28] The processions at the entrance and conclusion may be accompanied by a didgeridoo. The Aboriginal Our Father may be used "if appropriate" to the local Aboriginal community. (The one prepared by the Diocese of Broome begins, "You are our Father, You live in Heaven / We talk to you, Father, You are good.") A message stick can be carried forward with the Book of the Gospels and held upright during its proclamation.

Predictably, in some parts of Australia inculturated liturgies continue, and in other parts they have diminished. Still, the music, ritual, and prayers have promoted continuing reflection on the Eucharist not only among the Aboriginals themselves but also among the rest of the Catholic community, which honors their contributions on a special Sunday each year. The Mass belongs to the entire church, and the church inculturates the Mass.

Anglican Use

Episcopalians in the United States seeking to be received into the full communion of the Catholic Church have the option of entering special worship communities. In 1980 Pope John Paul II asked the prefect of the Congregation for the Doctrine of the Faith to inform the National Conference of Catholic Bishops (NCCB) that he was authorizing a special pastoral provision. The provision applies to both laity and clergy. If they qualify, married former Episcopal priests and bishops may be ordained Catholic priests. These priests, who are ordained for service in a particular Catholic diocese, may have personal worship communities to celebrate the Roman liturgy with some elements of the Anglican liturgy.[29]

The Congregation for Divine Worship established a special liturgical commission with the help of the Congregation for the Sacraments and Divine Worship in 1983. This group gathered into Roman usage some elements from the Anglican *Book of Common Prayer*. This led to the publication of the Catholic *Book of Divine Worship* from Newman House Press in 2003.[30] For the eucharistic prayer, the book adopted the Old English Translation of the Roman Canon, which begins, "Most merciful Father, we humbly pray thee, through Jesus Christ thy Son our Lord."[31] Although the words differ from both the first and second English translations in the Roman Rite, this canon otherwise carried over the rubrics, acclamations, and abbreviations to the Roman Canon (Eucharistic Prayer I) of the post–Vatican II Roman Missal. One theory about the Old English translation is that it is the work of the Protestant reformer William Tyndale (+1536), who translated the Latin canon into English in order to show its theological deficiencies. If so, it is ironic that his work is devoutly prayed by some former Episcopal priests received into Roman Catholicism.

Many of these former Episcopalians were probably already familiar with Anglican prayer books derived from Catholic sources. *The People's Anglican Missal in the American Edition*,[32] published in 1946, was the American counterpart to the *Anglican Missal*, first published in England in 1921.[33] These books descended not from the Anglican Book of Common Prayer, but from the Roman Missal. They originated and remain in use among some Anglo-Catholics, that is, among some Anglican congregations who preferred more elements of the Roman tradition. So, whereas Newman House Press's *Book of Divine Worship* was serving the needs of American Roman Catholics with Episcopal traditions, the *Anglican Missal* served the needs of American Episcopalians with Roman tendencies.

John Paul's pastoral provision for the United States prepared the way for Pope Benedict XVI's Apostolic Constitution *Anglicanorum cœtibus* in 2009.[34] According to its subtitle, Benedict's constitution provided "for Personal Ordinariates for Anglicans Entering into Full Communion with[35] the Catholic Church." The prevailing previous example of this structure is the military ordinariate, which has some properties of a diocese without inhabiting finite territory contiguous with other dioceses. The ordinariates that Benedict approved are erected within entire episcopal conferences and in consultation with them. Priests of the ordinariate work within dioceses, but they are priests of the ordinariate, not of the diocese. Liturgical celebrations may take place according to the books of the Roman Rite or "according to the liturgical books proper to the Anglican tradition, which have been approved by the Holy See, so as to maintain the liturgical, spiritual and pastoral traditions of the Anglican Communion within the Catholic Church, as a precious gift nourishing the faith of the members of the Ordinariate and as a treasure to be shared."[36]

To obtain books "approved by the Holy See," the Vatican undertook a revision of the 2003 American Catholic *Book of Divine Worship* in order to develop a resource suitable also to other countries outside the United States, notably England, Wales, Canada, and Australia. The idea was to blend Anglican traditions with both preconciliar and postconciliar Roman traditions. The book was first distributed in two loose-leaf volumes in 2013. In the United States these two volumes effectively replace the *Book of Divine Worship*. The first volume contains the Order of Mass, and the second contains supplemental texts, such as the presidential prayers for a given day or liturgical time. The two binders were considered interim until the revised book could be published, presumably under the same title as the *Book of Divine Worship*. The title is perhaps a Catholic rejoinder to the title of the Anglican *Book of Common Prayer*, with a nod to the name of the branch of the Roman curia responsible for liturgical work today, the Congregation for Divine Worship and the Discipline of the Sacraments.

A summary and explanation of the revised Order of Mass for the ordinariate is widely available,[37] but the complete texts were not distributed to the general public. Printed sheets were given to ordinariate parishes to place in binders, emphasizing the interim nature of the work. The underlying principles of the revision include the preservation of "the Anglican liturgical patrimony . . . [that] has nourished the Catholic faith," "to minimize the number of options," and to promote the sanctification and unity of the faithful coming to the Catholic Church from the Anglican tradition, a unity to be achieved among themselves, with other Catholics, and "with the See of Peter."

The ordinariate's Holy Mass begins with the sign of the cross, as the Roman Rite does. Prayers of preparation may be offered in the sacristy or at the foot of the altar, resembling a preconciliar custom. The greeting of the people comes just before the collect, as in the preconciliar Roman Rite. The Liturgy of the Word follows, according to the postconciliar Roman Lectionary for Mass: two readings and a psalm precede the proclamation of the gospel. The Revised Standard Version Catholic translation is commonly used, rather than the New American Bible, Revised Edition. After the homily all proclaim the Nicene Creed; there is no option for the Apostles' Creed as in the Roman Rite.

The penitential act is moved from the introductory rites to the conclusion of the "prayers of the people" at the end of the Liturgy of the Word, in keeping with classic Anglican eucharistic liturgies. Seven forms of the prayers of the people are provided; the first two are said by the priest alone—which deviates from the Roman prayer of the faithful—because they derive from the intercessions in the Roman Canon. The bidding for the penitential rite comes from the Anglican tradition: "Ye that do truly and earnestly repent you of your sins . . ." An alternate form similarly draws from Anglican vocabulary: "meekly kneeling upon your knees." The "comfortable words," a Cranmerian staple in the *Book of Common Prayer* that chains together a series of biblical passages, is retained in full.

"Sentences" function as a biblical bidding for the collection. For the preparation of the altar and the gifts, two forms are given, one inspired by the Anglican *Book of Common Prayer* and the other from the postconciliar Roman tradition. At the *Orate Fratres*, the priest begins, "Pray, brethren, that our sacrifice," instead of the more literal and theologically precise "my sacrifice and yours" from the revised English translation of the Roman Rite. (More on this below.) The posture of the faithful at this time matches the Roman custom.

In addition to the Old English translation of the Roman Canon, an Elizabethan-language version of Eucharistic Prayer II is offered as an option for weekdays. For the preface dialogue, the people stand as in the Roman tradition. Then they bow at the beginning of the Sanctus and rise to make the sign of the cross at the Benedictus, in keeping with the Anglican custom. The translation of the Sanctus replaces the first Hosanna with "Glory be to thee, O Lord Most High." People kneel after the Sanctus as they do in the Roman Rite in the United States. The first two options for the memorial acclamation come directly from the revised translation of the Roman Rite, while the third comes from the *Book of Common Prayer*'s Office for the Visitation of the Sick, just before the handlaying: "O Saviour of the world, who by thy Cross and precious Blood hast redeemed us: save us and help us, we humbly beseech thee, O Lord."

After the eucharistic prayer, the people stand for the Lord's Prayer, as in Roman usage. The bidding draws from the *Book of Common Prayer*: "As our Saviour Christ hath commanded and taught us, we are bold to say." The Lord's Prayer in Anglican usage concludes with the doxology "For Thine is the kingdom . . . ," but this Order of Mass imitates the Roman practice, which inserts an embolism before that acclamation. The Ordinariate's embolism draws from the Anglican missal traditions: "Deliver us, O Lord, we beseech thee, from all evils, past, present, and to come." The sign of peace follows the Lord's Prayer as in the Roman Rite. The people remain kneeling from this time throughout Communion, which more nearly imitates a Roman custom. The priest says a devotional prayer before receiving Communion, his hands joined and placed on the altar, according to the preconciliar Roman rubric. The prayer of humble access, preliminary to receiving Communion in the *Book of Common Prayer*, is offered in full. The invitation to Communion comes from the Roman tradition: "Behold the Lamb of God, Behold him that taketh away. . . ." While administering Communion, the minister uses a formula from the earliest *Book of Common Prayer*: "The Body of our Lord Jesus Christ, which was given for thee, preserve thy body and soul unto everlasting life." A slight variation is said for receiving from the cup and when both kinds are administered together. The congregation recites a thanksgiving prayer after Communion, which also comes from the *Book of Common Prayer*. Then the priest says the post-communion prayer as in the Roman Rite. The proclamation of the Last Gospel, which was obligatory in the preconciliar Roman Rite, is made optional.

These adaptations to the Roman Rite are in use for those former Anglicans who are part of the ordinariate and who prefer them over the Roman Rite. The vast majority of Episcopalians becoming Catholic prefer the Roman Rite, so the usage of these adaptations is fairly limited. The goal was to grant "legitimate diversity in the expression of our common faith."[38] The result is not an Anglican Rite but an Anglican expression of the one Roman Rite. Still, when wondering "Whose Mass is it?" the answer is broad enough to accommodate a significant group with its own liturgical patrimony and contemporary liturgical preferences. The Roman Rite is not as uniform as many people think.

Protestant Reforms

The changes to the Catholic Mass did not produce equivalent changes in Protestant congregations because the most dramatic differences did not apply. The order of service had not remained virtually unchanged for hundreds of years. Vernacular languages were already in use. Changing to a freestanding altar did not pertain. What did appeal to Protestant groups was the ecumenical climate. The Second Vatican Council's Decree on Ecumenism[39] praised common prayer among Christians: "It is allowable, indeed desirable that Catholics should join in prayer with their separated brethren. Such prayers in common are certainly an effective means of obtaining the grace of unity, and they are a true expression of the ties which still bind Catholics to their separated brethren."[40]

One unexpected tie developed in the use of a lectionary. The Liturgy of the Word at the preconciliar Catholic Mass typically included an epistle and a gospel. Rarely did a reading come from the Old Testament. Always the readings had been in Latin. With the revision of the Lectionary, Catholics now hear on Sundays a three-year cycle of three readings plus a psalm in the vernacular, the first reading consistently from the Old Testament except during Easter Time. The weekdays, which formerly repeated the Sunday readings, now have their own two-year cycle. Catholics are hearing a richer share of the biblical treasure than ever before.

This caught the attention of many other churches, especially in North America. Several Christian churches independently worked on their own lectionary, inspired by the Catholic model. The Consultation on Common Texts, an ecumenical body representing Christian churches in the United States and Canada, began to harmonize and rework these diverse examples into a single whole.[41] They then joined with an international body, the English Language Liturgical Consultation, to produce the Revised Common Lectionary. This resource supplied a series of readings suitable for Sunday worship, arranged on a three-year cycle of three readings plus a psalm. The Revised Common Lectionary diverges at places from the Roman collection, but Christians around the world hear a more harmonious proclamation of readings on Sundays than they ever have in the past.

Whereas the lectionary consensus was unexpected, a deliberate ecumenical effort produced a single English translation of other elements shared in Sunday eucharistic worship. These elements, taken from what Catholics call the Order of Mass, led ICEL to consult with other Christian traditions starting in 1967. By 1968 these meetings had produced common translations of the Nicene Creed, the Apostles' Creed, the Lord's Prayer, and some liturgical dialogues.[42] In 1969 this advisory body had come to be known as the International Consultation on English Texts (ICET), and the agreement on translations expanded even further to include such parts of Sunday worship as the Gloria, the Sanctus, the memorial acclamations, and the Agnus Dei.[43] In 1993 Bishop Wilton Gregory explained these efforts in his address to the NCCB: "The Apostolic See had encouraged such cooperative ecumenical efforts, as is noted in the recently published Ecumenical Directory from Rome. These texts are the ecumenical versions of the Gloria, Creed, Sanctus, and Lord's Prayer. Each conference of bishops is free to use these texts or not. In the United States, we have used these ecumenical texts with the exception of the Lord's Prayer, since the late 1960's."[44]

These achievements supported the ecumenical dialogue by giving Christians common words to say when they gathered together in Christ. For example, the *Lutheran Book of Worship*[45] and the Presbyterian *Book of Common Worship*[46] share many of the ICET texts that were adopted for the Roman Catholic Sacramentary. Examples can also be found in the *United Methodist Book of Worship*[47] and *A New Zealand Prayer Book / He Karakia Mihinare o Aotearoa*.[48] Even the Episcopal *Book of Common Prayer* shares some of the common texts.[49]

Between the Lectionary and the ICET texts, Catholic and Protestant liturgies shared elements that underscored their common Christian faith. They forged a foundation from which hopes of greater unity emerged. As will be seen, when changes happened to the English-language texts in the Roman Missal, they shook the trust in this ecumenical foundation. Only later did it become evident how much other Christians had invested in the Catholic Mass.

WomenEucharist

Ordination to the Catholic priesthood is limited to males.[50] Pope John Paul II used strong language in his Apostolic Letter *Ordinatio sacerdotalis* to drive home the point: "I declare that the Church has no authority whatsoever to confer priestly ordination on women and that this judgment is to be definitively held by all the Church's faithful."[51]

Some individuals and groups who resolutely identify themselves as Catholic have formed communities that accept the ordination of women. The official Roman position is that such ordinations are invalid, and the participants who simulate ordination are excommunicated. Dissenting from this view, members of groups such as the Women's Ordination Conference[52] consider themselves part of the Catholic Church.

Of interest to this study is that the eucharistic ceremonies celebrated by participants within the women's ordination movement largely derive from the Roman Catholic Mass. As the Mass inspired the ceremonies of Protestants and Anglicans, so it inspires those who actively support the ordination of women.

Some of these groups gather regularly for informal worship, and some boast a number of long-term faithful participants. One study in 1997 identified over one hundred WomenEucharist groups meeting at least once a month within the United States, and participants in dozens of them agreed to be interviewed.[53] Members of a group generally meet in a home or meeting room and sit in a circle. Leadership is shared, rather than assigned to one member. A eucharistic prayer may be read by all participants together. Spoken words are gender-inclusive; the liturgy is Cristocentric. The worship is based on biblical and eucharistic traditions. In a typical WomenEucharist group, men do not participate. Many members also maintain their participation in a Roman Catholic parish, though they find additional value in their separate meeting. Groups may use the prayers and Scripture readings that could be heard at the local Catholic church. Or they may improvise prayers or use additional resources, even for the readings.

One resource, *Inclusive Worship Aids*,[54] supplies a dozen different samples. These generally follow a similar pattern, easily recognizable by those familiar with the Catholic Mass. The service opens with a gathering song and greeting. One example of the penitential rite is based on the formula for sacramental absolution in the Roman Rite, but recited by all. After the opening prayer comes a version of the Gloria. The Liturgy of the Word may present two readings, a psalm, and a gospel. A homily is preached, and then all recite a profession of faith—though not the one from Nicaea. This one opens with a brief treatment of the Trinity and then moves into other statements of belief: "We believe that God loves us passionately. . . . We believe in the partnership and equality of women and men. . . . We believe that women's liberation is human liberation." Then come the general intercessions and the preparation of the gifts. The eucharistic prayer is to be shared by two alternating voices. It includes statements of praise and petition, the institution narrative (in which all present recite together the consecratory words of Jesus), and the invocation of saints. These sample eucharistic prayers do not share the Roman Catholic emphasis on the offering of selves in union with the offering of Christ. The Lord's Prayer is to begin "Our Father and Mother." Then come the sign of peace and the breaking of bread, Communion and the prayer after Communion. In the concluding rite all recite a blessing together, the presider dismisses the group, and all sing a closing hymn.

Throughout, forms of address for God are gender-inclusive or gender-neutral. Militant and hierarchical language common to Roman liturgical prayer is replaced with milder images. Thus, although the structure of the service is recognizable by those familiar with the Roman Rite, the content, vocabulary, and purpose of the prayers are different. This is but one resource, and the women's eucharistic groups are quite diverse. Yet the members seem to treasure a eucharistic resemblance to the traditional structure of the Roman Catholic Mass.

Outside these small groups, some adherents of women's ordination have formed larger social units patterned on parishes of a Roman Catholic diocese. An example of this movement is the Ecumenical Catholic Church.[55] Both men and women are eligible for ordination within this organization. Membership generally appeals to people who do not feel welcomed elsewhere—women, LGBTs, the divorced and remarried, those with gluten intolerance, people who sympathize with the needs of those groups, and theological outliers. The Ecumenical Catholic Church aims to provide a broad-based welcome. A typical Sunday service uses the same three-year Lectionary for Mass as found in Roman Rite parishes. Prayers are read from the Sacramentary—the first English translation of the Roman Missal. These prayers are stylistically easier to comprehend than those in the revised translation; however, the Sacramentary prayers have much gender-exclusive language that leaders revise.

The liturgies of the women's ordination movement show both affinity with and divergence from the Roman Rite. Proponents appreciate the overall structure of the Mass—the proclamation of Scriptures and the continuance of a eucharistic tradition. But they have assumed ownership over the language of the prayers, alternative structural elements, and the role of women in leadership. Canonically, these liturgies are considered invalid.

Society of Saint Pius X

Staking a different claim to the Roman liturgy are groups that prefer the preconciliar to the postconciliar Mass. Some of these take the extreme position that the postconciliar Mass is not a true expression of Catholicism; others are more conciliatory. The most renowned adherent to the preconciliar liturgy is the Society of Saint Pius X (SSPX), founded by Archbishop Marcel Lefebvre (+1991).

The hallmarks of the preconciliar Mass include the use of the Latin language, the allowance of only the Roman Canon for the eucharistic prayer, the omission of the prayer of the faithful and the sign of peace, the reduction in size of the Lectionary, and a more limited participation of the people. The liturgy of this group restores repetitions and structures that were simplified after the council. It also observes the preconciliar liturgical calendar.

In the case of SSPX, its ideology expands beyond the liturgy. It lists among its concerns "modernism," "religious liberty," "ecumenism," "collegiality," and "liturgical abuses."[56] The liturgy is only one component of a spirituality driven by a preconciliar worldview.

Producing the greatest difficulty, Lefebvre conferred an "unlawful episcopal ordination"[57] on four priests in 1988. The action provoked an immediate rebuke from Pope John Paul II, who confirmed that all five clerics had "incurred the grave penalty of excommunication."[58] Archbishop Lefebvre died in 1991, but in 2009, in a failed effort to heal the division, the Congregation for Bishops with the approval of Pope Benedict XVI lifted the excommunication of the four bishops whom Lefebvre had ordained.[59] Yet Pope Benedict also clarified that the ministers of the society "do not exercise legitimate ministries in the Church."[60] In 2013 Cardinal Gerhard Müller, the prefect for the Congregation for the Doctrine of the Faith, declared in an interview that the bishops ordained by Archbishop Lefebvre are in schism.[61]

The society does not see it that way. Its mission "is to preserve the Catholic faith in its fullness and purity, to teach its truths, and to diffuse its virtues, especially through the Roman Catholic Priesthood. Authentic spiritual life, the sacraments, and the traditional liturgy are its primary means of bringing this life of grace to souls."[62] Its self-perception vis-a-vis mainstream Catholicism and the goals orienting its work share surprising parallels with the Women's Ordination Conference, which aims "to reclaim the early Christianity tradition of a discipleship of equals" with a focus on priesthood.[63] From the Vatican's perspective, both groups condone unlawful ordinations.

Confusing many Catholics was Pope Benedict's decision in 2007 to allow more broadly a legitimate celebration of the very same preconciliar Mass under certain circumstances. These include "parishes where a group of the faithful attached to the previous liturgical tradition stably exists."[64] Consequently, some celebrations of the preconciliar Mass take place in union with the church; others do not. The liturgy is the same.

Adherents to the preconciliar liturgy maintain a spirit of autonomy in light of the reforms following the Second Vatican Council. They are among the many groups and individuals who claim some ownership of the Roman Catholic Mass.

Eastern Rites

Eastern Churches generally divide between Orthodox and Catholic, that is, some who are not in union with Rome and some who are. Each has its own divine liturgy, and all of these relate more to each other than to the Roman Rite. If asking, "Whose Mass is it?" to members of these churches, they would all probably answer, "Well, not ours."

Yet the Eastern rites have had an impact on the celebration of the Catholic Mass. As indicated above, the epiclesis was introduced into the Roman eucharistic prayer after the Second Vatican Council because of its centrality in the Eastern anaphoras. The only exceptions are Eucharistic Prayer I (the Roman Canon), which has no explicit epiclesis, and the Eucharistic Prayers for Masses with Children, which were initially composed without an epiclesis. When the first English translation was being prepared, translators added an epiclesis to each of the children's eucharistic prayers, and the Vatican approved them all. Now the epiclesis appears even in the "original" Latin of these prayers.

The difference, as indicated above, is the location of the epiclesis, which precedes the institution narrative in the Roman Rite. Nonetheless, it is there, and it wouldn't be there had it not been for the influence of the East.

Another Eastern feature of postconciliar eucharistic prayers is the memorial acclamation. Prior to the council, the only acclamation resounding within the Roman Canon was the Sanctus. Yet for many centuries, it was largely considered preliminary to, rather than constitutive of, the Canon. The Eastern Rites traditionally include more acclamations of the people throughout the anaphora. The Roman study group preparing the revised Order of Mass after the council added three versions of an acclamation that could be made after the consecration. The first of these ("We proclaim your Death, O Lord . . .") was lifted from the Antiochene Anaphora of Saint James, the Brother of the Lord.[65]

The same study group had proposed adding an entire eucharistic prayer from the Eastern traditions, the Anaphora of Saint Basil.[66] This would have given the Christian world one eucharistic prayer shared by many churches East and West. The location of the epiclesis, however, proved a difficulty too great for some of the group to overcome, and the addition of this anaphora to the Roman Catholic Mass lost by one vote. In its place, the group composed what came to be known as Eucharistic Prayer IV, which shares affinity with ancient Eastern sources, though it is a new Western composition.

In celebrating marriage, the nuptial blessings of the Roman Rite now include an epiclesis over the couple. This has been an important feature in the East, where the blessing of the priest confers the sacrament. In the Roman Rite, where there had never been an epiclesis, the couple themselves confer the sacrament by reciting to each other the words of consent. The third edition of the Roman Missal added an epiclesis to the Latin of the nuptial blessings in 2002, and these appeared in English for the first time in 2011.

Not to be overlooked is the contribution that Eastern Rites made to the debate of celebrating Mass in vernacular languages. The vernacular has been in use consistently throughout the history of the various churches of the East.

The Eastern Rites did not directly claim any ownership of the Roman Mass, but their point of view was taken into account in many developments of the Roman liturgy after Vatican II.

Conclusions

Like a musical theme and variation, the Roman Catholic Mass has inspired different groups to introduce modifications to their worship. In some way each group has answered "ours" to the question, "Whose Mass is it?"

- Some non-European nations and cultures have introduced adaptations to the structure and content of Sunday worship.

- Some of those joining the Catholic Church from Anglican communities have incorporated some of the liturgical patrimony that formed their faith into the Roman Mass.

- Some Protestant churches adopted some features of the Roman Mass into their worship, which strengthened affinities with the Roman Rite, while creating a sense of respectful sharing in elements of the Order of Mass.

- Some women's groups sought and implemented further changes to the postconciliar Mass to emphasize values of equality, welcome, and creativity.

- Some Catholics rejected the liturgical reforms of the Second Vatican Council and returned to preconciliar worship patterns.

- The Eastern Rites, through the constancy of their traditions and the richness of their liturgical theology, inspired some changes to the Mass.

The postconciliar changes to the Mass untethered a variety of groups to develop further adaptations to address their local needs.

The Vatican's Authority

Contrasting with the impulse to explore variations on the official Roman Rite in the decades after the council, the Vatican asserted ever greater authority over ever more minute details in the celebration of the Mass. Whereas the council supported the socio-economic principle of subsidiarity,[1] the postconciliar era witnessed a greater centralization of authority in the Roman pontiff and his curia. This especially pertained to the realm of liturgy.

Sacramentaries and Missals

The very existence of sacramentaries, missals, and lectionaries indicates the centralizing principle of the liturgy. Many Catholics feel proud that the Mass is practically the same no matter whether they pray in their home diocese or around the world. They can spot differences, of course, but they feel at home with the similarities. The trend can be traced at least to the early Middle Ages.

In the early centuries of Christianity, it was virtually impossible to codify liturgical books. Liturgies were improvised. Various practices coexisted among the diverse urban centers of Christian growth. The written word was expensive and rare. Communication among bishops was arduous.

As mentioned above, however, by the early Middle Ages, the desire to collect liturgical resources and the capability of compiling them blossomed. The sixth-century Verona Sacramentary contains a host of material that was probably composed at least a century before. It is not a complete liturgical book. It opens in April—the material for January, February, and March has never been found—and it includes only presidential prayers such as the collect, the secret (prayer over the offerings), and the prayer after Communion. It also includes some prefaces and prayers over the people. It describes no order of Mass, rubrics, dialogues, or eucharistic prayer. These surely existed in practice, but written evidence is sparse. The editor compiled what was findable. The book ascribes one collection of Mass texts per day, but on some days there are more. The prayers were written in Rome, but the only surviving copy of the collection came to light in eighteenth-century Verona. An early commentator believed it was the work of Pope Leo the Great; hence it is sometimes called either the Leonine Sacramentary or the Verona Sacramentary, even though it does not have all the components that a sacramentary is expected to have. By preserving and sharing prayers originating in and around Rome, the Verona Sacramentary began the process of compiling a book to be shared from Rome with the rest of the Catholic world.

The Gelasian Sacramentary, compiled in France by the mid-eighth century, preserved more of the developing Roman tradition along with Gallican customs. By the mid-ninth century the Gregorian Sacramentary had advanced from Rome across the Alps into other territories. The Franks put their own adaptations onto the liturgy, amplifying its ceremonies, and these were brought back into Rome with the tenth-century Roman-Germanic Pontifical. Several other Roman Pontificals elaborated on these traditions, which laid the groundwork for the first edition of the Roman Missal in 1474.

The Council of Trent had a further impact on centralizing the liturgy. In a reaction to the growing Protestant Reformation, the Roman Missal was reissued in 1570, and other rites were gathered into the Roman Ritual in 1614. The Roman Missal included the presidential prayers, antiphons, and readings for each day, along with an Order of Mass and a select number of prefaces to be used at the head of the Roman Canon. The Mass remained virtually the same throughout a span of four centuries in every country of the Catholic world. Read in Latin, it was managed by detailed rubrics. In practice, the execution surely lacked idealized uniformity, but the book remained virtually the same.

After the Second Vatican Council, when Pope Paul VI authorized the revised Roman Missal in 1970, four hundred years had elapsed since the publication of the Roman Missal that followed the Council of Trent. The changes he introduced to the Missal were also an exercise of Vatican authority, but—except for a small percentage—the faithful broadly welcomed the revisions, especially because of the vernacular.

The Lectionary for Mass

A preamble to the intense discussions about the second English translation of the postconciliar Missal can be discerned in the 1998 publication of the second edition of the Lectionary for Mass in the United States. Here can be traced the Vatican's growing exercise of authority over the revised liturgical books in the decades after their introduction.

The first English lectionaries were produced in 1970, as the Latin typical edition of the entire Missal was becoming available. As the revised Order of Mass was being implemented, so was its lectionary. Outside the United States, the English translation of the Jerusalem Bible was approved for countries such as Australia, England, Ireland, New Zealand, Pakistan, Scotland, South Africa, and Wales. In India, Catholics could choose between the Jerusalem Bible and the Revised Standard Version, which had been approved for Canada. The New American Bible was accepted for use in the Philippines. Inside the United States three translations were initially approved: the New American Bible, the Revised Standard Version, and the Jerusalem Bible.[2]

Work on a second edition of the Lectionary began after the Vatican issued a second Latin edition in 1981. By that time, the shortcomings of the first English edition were becoming apparent. The passages were printed in paragraph blocks, not in sense lines. The wide use of gender-exclusive terms was broadly criticized. The English translation of the Jerusalem Bible depended on the French, which had used some freedoms of expression. Also, the Consultation on Common Texts had prepared a variation of the order of readings for Christian bodies outside the Catholic Church, and the subcommittee working on the revised Catholic Lectionary studied that work as well.[3]

Gender-exclusive language proved to be the thorniest issue. The American bishops established a special Joint Committee on Exclusive Language, drawing from the membership of their committees on liturgy and doctrine. Over a three-year period this group worked on a response to the rising concerns. In November 1990, the plenary assembly of the NCCB approved the joint committee's "Criteria for Evaluation of Inclusive Language Translations of Scripture Texts Proposed for Liturgical Use."[4] These criteria established two general principles: fidelity to the Word of God, which it obviously deemed primary, and respect for the nature of the liturgical assembly. They called for the replacement of words such as "men," "sons," "brothers," "brethren," "forefathers," "fraternity," and "brotherhood" with ones that are more gender-inclusive. They favored the use of masculine pronouns for God, as the Bible does. They requested, however, that divine feminine imagery in the original, such as in the Wisdom literature, not be obscured. The bishops' criteria retained the traditional names of the Trinity, as well as the masculine pronoun for the Holy Spirit. In reference to the church, they sanctioned the third-person neuter singular pronoun (it), or the third-person plural pronoun (they).

In 1992, the bishops approved not only a revised translation of the Lectionary for Mass using the New American Bible (NAB) but also one using the New Revised Standard Version (NRSV), which the Vatican had approved for Canada. The American bishops also adopted the Contemporary English Version of the Bible for use in the Lectionary for Masses with Children.[5]

The Canadian bishops had received approval to use the NRSV, so they published a lectionary with that translation in 1992. They had not, however, submitted a complete draft to the Vatican for approval. Assuming that it had obtained sufficient authority, the Canadian conference printed the Lectionary without a letter of approval from the Vatican among its opening pages. This eventually caused difficulties in Canada.

The American bishops wanted to publish two different translations together: the NAB and the NRSV.[6] This decision provoked considerable discussion over some years, but as late as 1994 the Bishops' Committee on the Liturgy (BCL) decided not to publish one translation without the other.[7] The delay permitted the Vatican to exercise greater scrutiny on the project. Bishop Donald Trautman, then chairman of the Bishops' Committee on the Liturgy, told members of the Federation of Diocesan Liturgical Commissions, "You should not be surprised to learn that the difficulties encountered with the approval of the English translation of the Catechism have had their effect on the NAB Lectionary."[8]

The Catechism had first appeared in French, the language of its composition, in 1992. The conference of American bishops developed an English translation and submitted it to the Congregation for the Doctrine of the Faith. Approval did not come. The submitted translation chose gender-inclusive words and the style of translation encouraged by *Comme le prévoit*, but the Vatican rejected this approach and prepared its own version. Translations into other major languages were available almost immediately when the Catechism was promulgated, but the English did not appear until 1994.[9] The published translation was different from the one the bishops had submitted.

In 1994 Bishop Trautman explained that efforts were underway with two congregations in Rome to resolve issues pertaining to the Lectionary.[10] Surprisingly, the CDWDS had recently rescinded the approval of the NRSV[11] and raised many issues concerning the translation of NAB. This led to an unprecedented consultation in Rome with "a small group of bishops and Scripture scholars" in January 1995 to discuss issues pertaining to the Lectionary.[12] Trautman said later that year, "Although I cannot go into details about the *Lectionary for Mass*, I can tell you that the discussions with the Congregation for the Doctrine of the Faith are progressing and that I and several other bishops with degrees in biblical studies are carefully going through the text and will be proposing some revisions to the Congregation."[13] The bishops abandoned their plan to publish two lectionaries and settled on only one, drawn from the NAB.

After the special January consultation, the Congregation for the Doctrine of the Faith issued to the participants its norms for the translation of biblical texts in the liturgy. These became known as the "secret norms" because they were not shared beyond the group. They were made public, however, in 1997.[14] The opening principle summarized the goals: "The Church must always seek to convey accurately in translation the texts she has inherited from the biblical, liturgical, and patristic tradition and instruct the faithful in their proper meaning." The norms then requested "maximum possible fidelity to the words of the text," even if they have an "inelegant mode of human expression." They called for special care that "a Christological meaning is not precluded." The implications were serious: "Thus, the word 'man' in English should as a rule translate 'adam and anthropos, since there is no one synonym which effectively conveys the play between the individual, the collectivity and the unity of the human family so important, for example, to expression of Christian doctrine and anthropology."

The bishops of the United States reworked the first volume of the Lectionary in 1997, approved it, and submitted it to the Vatican for approval. At the same time, the Secretariat for the Liturgy made available to the bishops an extensive commentary on the revision of the Lectionary.[15] It was almost entirely consumed by the issue of gender-exclusive language. The Lectionary contained excerpts from the 1970 Old Testament of the NAB and the 1986 revised New Testament. The commentary then explained the various ways that the Greek words formerly rendered as "brother," "son," and "man" were being handled, along with the usage of the masculine pronouns in general. Some editorial changes were also noted. Within months the CDWDS confirmed the first volume for use in the United States.[16]

The translation of the Psalms also supplied some drama. Originally the Grail Psalter was approved for the Liturgy of the Hours, while the NAB Psalter served the other liturgical books, including the Lectionary. A committee revised the NAB Psalter some years later, and the American bishops approved it for the Lectionary in 1992. The Vatican rejected the revised translation, however, when it rescinded the permissions for the NRSV in 1994.[17] ICEL had produced its own Psalter the same year, creating a translation that thoroughly employed gender-neutral vocabulary for pronouns referring to human beings and even for pronouns pertaining to God.[18] The ICEL Psalter was never approved by the Vatican for liturgical usage. Eventually a revised Grail Psalter was approved, but only after much debate.

The Grail had a simple origin. A group of Roman Catholic laywomen in England formed a secular institute for the purposes of prayer, companionship, and service. Their official title is The Women of Nazareth, known as the Grail.[19] For the purposes of their daily prayer, the society published its own translation of the Psalms in

1963. Using a sprung rhythm that imitated the pulses of the original Hebrew, the translation especially fit the music composed by the French Jesuit Joseph Gelineau.[20] Many of these settings appeared in English-language participation aids after the council, where their popularity grew. In 1974 the NCCB approved the Grail Psalms for the first English translation of the Liturgy of the Hours.

The BCL revised the Grail Psalter for inclusive language in 1984, but it failed to win the conference's approval. In 1998 the BCL asked Abbot Gregory Polan of Conception Abbey, Missouri, to work on a new revised translation of the Grail Psalter from the Hebrew.[21] Abbot Gregory and other monks of the abbey set about the work.

With the publication of new translation rules in *Liturgiam authenticam* (see below), the Committee on Scripture Translations proposed a revision to the NAB Psalter, and the BCL encouraged Abbot Gregory to complete the work on the revised Grail. Both the revised NAB and the revised Grail were submitted to the Committee on Scripture Translations for review in 2003. In 2006 that committee recommended the Grail, praising the quality of its revision for biblical faithfulness, poetic beauty, and musical suitability. Within months the BCL's Subcommittee on Music and the Liturgy made the same recommendation.

In June 2008, the conference voted on the two Psalters.[22] Ten years after the BCL originally proposed the project to Abbot Gregory, the bishops chose his revised Grail. It still had to be submitted, however, to the CDWDS. Approval came in 2010, but only after the CDWDS introduced a number of changes—some of which created problems of consistency and rhythm.

This approved revised Grail Psalter provided a reference for translating sections of the third edition of the Roman Missal, such as the antiphons for days in the liturgical year, as well as the psalms for the procession of Palm Sunday of the Lord's Passion. While the American bishops were considering translations of other parts of the Liturgy of the Hours in 2014, however, they took another look at the revised Grail. As the *Newsletter* notes about the events in 2010, "The translation [of the Revised Grail] came back to the Bishops from Rome with some corrections. A 'revision of the revision' will be before the Bishops in November."[23] The bishops approved the revised revision for inclusion in all liturgical books in the United States.

When dealing with any book of the Bible, translators are facing the Word of God. Strong opinions will be expressed, as they should. It is important to get the Word right. The Vatican's concern over the biblical translation soon shifted to the Roman Missal, where it further exercised its authority over the words of the Mass.

The Revised Sacramentary

After the postconciliar Mass first became available in Latin in 1969 and 1970, ICEL completed its work on the Sacramentary (the Roman Missal) in 1972. The books were published in several countries, including the United States, in 1974. Almost immediately, some revisions were proposed, and the bishops of the United States published a second edition of the Sacramentary in 1985. One of its revisions pertained to the words of consecration. The 1974 Sacramentary had the priest quote Jesus saying of his blood, "It will be shed for you and for all men." The 1985 Sacramentary deleted the word "men." The pastoral concern for gender-inclusive language had reached the heart of the eucharistic prayer.

Meanwhile, ICEL had begun a more serious revision of the entire Sacramentary. By its own admission the first translation was done quickly to accommodate the urgent need for a Mass in the vernacular. So in 1982, the commission began a year-long consultation, followed by the long process of revising 1,324 prayers.[24] The effort drew the translation closer to the Latin originals while building on the prayerful, communicative style that ICEL had been developing. Bishop Joseph Delaney reported on the progress to the bishops of the United States in 1989, praising the quality of the work: "ICEL has done a fine job in revising the translations, and we all can look forward to this new English edition of the *Roman Missal*."[25] The American bishops voted on the final segments of the work in 1996,[26] and it finally passed in 1997 with minor revisions.[27] Every one of ICEL's eleven member conferences of bishops approved the work with unanimous or near-unanimous votes.[28] After fifteen years of work, the revised Sacramentary had reached the CDWDS.

It was not welcome. The Vatican had already rejected translations of a catechism, a lectionary, a psalter, and revised ordination rites. The changing mood became evident when Chicago's Cardinal Francis

George told fellow members of ICEL that the Vatican had ordered far-reaching changes in the direction of ICEL's work and its very organizational plan.[29] In 2002, finally responding to conferences who had submitted the revised translation of the Sacramentary, the CDWDS decided that it was "regrettably unable to accord the *recognitio* to this text in the form in which it was submitted."[30] The pages of problems it delineated included the organization of the book, the inclusion of newly composed texts, grammar, sentence structure, inclusive language, vocabulary, content, and liturgical roles. The prefect of the congregation, Cardinal Jorge Medina Estévez, threatened "the withdrawal of any degree of approbation, presumed or explicit, of the present Mixed Commission by the Congregation,"[31] as well as "a thorough and genuine renewal of the personnel to be involved in the preparation and administration of any translation projects [of the commission] . . . together with the exclusion from the same projects of those individuals heretofore involved in similar projects."[32]

ICEL's own description of those years is more irenic: "In the late 1990s, the Holy See asked ICEL to reflect on its function and the structure that had steered the work of translation . . . and to evaluate whether changes in the structure of the organization were needed."[33]

From there it was a short step to the restructuring of ICEL's statutes, the publication of *Liturgiam authenticam*, and the establishment of a new advisory body, Vox Clara. When the Latin third edition of the Roman Missal was published in 2002, a reconstituted ICEL began work on the project with new rules for translation and new procedures for approval.

Liturgiam Authenticam

The CDWDS issued new norms for translation with its instruction *Liturgiam authenticam* (LA) in 2001.[34] This replaced the norms that had been in force up to that point, *Comme le prévoit* (CLP). The contrast between the two can be easily discerned. Where CLP said a translation cannot be judged on the basis of individual words but rather on the total context (6), LA said the text, "insofar as possible, must be translated integrally and in the most exact manner" (20). Where CLP said that the "unit of meaning" is not the individual word but the whole passage (12), LA said that the translator "should strive to maintain the denotation, or primary sense of the words and expressions found in the original text, as well as their connotation" (52). Where CLP said it is necessary to take into account not only the message but also the speaker, the audience, and the style (7), LA asked translators to maintain the "straightforward, concise and compact manner of expression" that the Roman Rite features (57). Where CLP urged translators to consider the Latin words in light of their cultural and Christian context (11), LA said that they "should not attempt to render too explicit that which is implicit in the original texts" (28). CLP called for language in "common" usage (15); LA says that "words or expressions are sometimes employed which differ somewhat from usual and everyday speech" (27). CLP says, "The prayer of the Church is always the prayer of some actual community, assembled here and now" (20), but LA says, "The liturgical texts should be considered as the voice of the Church at prayer, rather than of only particular congregations or individuals" (27). In some places, the influence of the "secret norms" from the Lectionary translation can be felt, especially in the way that LA disparages the trend toward gender-inclusive language (30–31).

Beyond these guidelines, the CDWDS set up its own advisory body for English-language translations: Vox Clara.[35] The CDWDS has to review translations in every language from around the world, so its members have different skills. Not everyone knows English, and the CDWDS thought it wise to have its own advisory body of English-speaking bishops to review the work that ICEL prepared for the conferences. Whereas ICEL serves the conferences of bishops, Vox Clara directly serves the CDWDS. Vox Clara remains an advisory body. The Congregation holds all final authority on liturgical texts: "For the good of the faithful, the Holy See reserves to itself the right to prepare translations in any language, and to approve them for liturgical use."[36] In their own view, they are shepherds looking after the flock.

Not everyone saw it that way. First, the Second Vatican Council had placed the responsibility for liturgical translations in the hands of the conferences of bishops. The work had normally been sent to Rome for a *recognitio*, but this was usually handled without much bother. Now, in the words of Peter Jeffery, something else was happening: "The most worrisome thing about *LA* is that what it lacks in factuality it makes up with naked aggression. It speaks words of power and control rather than cooperation and consultation, much less charity. Asserting a right to impose translations on episcopal conferences (104), or take charge of any translation that might be used in Rome itself (76) are the kind of thing I mean."[37]

Horace Allen, a Presbyterian liturgist participating in an ecumenical gathering on liturgy at Rome's Centro Pro Unione, delivered a withering epithet on the consequences of the revised rules of translation: "The entire ecumenical liturgical conversation and dialogue is over—finished, dead, done."[38] His bleak assessment was shared by others.

David Holeton, a professor at Charles University in Prague, echoed these sentiments in his address at the conference celebrating the fiftieth anniversary of the founding of Rome's Pontifical Liturgical Institute, Sant'Anselmo.[39] He cited *Liturgiam authenticam*'s treatment of prayers shared by other Christians. LA states, "Great caution is to be taken to avoid a wording or style that the Catholic faithful would confuse with the manner of speech of non-Catholic ecclesial communities or of other religions, so that such a factor will not cause them confusion or discomfort."[40] Many non-Catholic Christians find that sentence offensive. Holeton shared similar criticisms in his presidential address to Societas Liturgica at its Palermo meeting in 2007.[41]

Paul Westermeyer, professor of church music and cantor at Luther Seminary in St. Paul, Minnesota, wrote an open letter to Pope Benedict in 2009 to express his sadness over the forthcoming revisions to the Missal. The ecumenical movement had benefited from liturgical cooperation. Changes to the Catholic Order of Mass would jeopardize the benefits that a uniform translation had bestowed on many Christian communities that share some liturgical dialogues, hymns, and acclamations. Westermeyer wrote, "The common texts we have struggled so hard to figure out together are used by families who each week attend services in two heritages, one Roman Catholic and one perhaps Reformed, Lutheran, Methodist, or Episcopal. Some families don't attend services in both traditions, but they hear the same lectionary and confess the same Creed in separate services. These families will now be divided by different details of wording for the Ordinary, so that they will have difficulty speaking or singing common texts together any more."[42]

Maxwell Johnson, professor of liturgy at the University of Notre Dame and an ordained pastor of the Evangelical Lutheran Church in America, similarly highlighted the liturgical contributions to ecumenism, including the common texts for the "Lord, have mercy," "Glory to God," the Nicene Creed, dialogues, the "Holy, Holy, Holy," and the Lamb of God. The common lectionary is another great treasure, he recalls. Johnson wrote in 2009, however, that "the now-approved new translation of the Roman Catholic Order of Mass has put an end to this common liturgical language among English-speaking Christians, with the result that much of English-speaking Protestant Christianity alone will be using what was originally Roman Catholic liturgical language."[43] He shows that *Liturgiam authenticam* itself called for agreement in translations "also with the particular non-Catholic Eastern Churches or with the authorities of the Protestant ecclesial communities, provided that it is not a question of a liturgical text pertaining to doctrinal matters still in dispute."[44] Yet this did not happen with these commonly shared texts in English. Johnson's article is taken from a full lecture at Yale, where he also cited the "caution" that *Liturgiam authenticam* made concerning words emanating from non-Catholic sources.[45] As Johnson points out, these are often the same words used in *Catholic* worship after the council that *then* were placed into Protestant books.[46]

At meetings of the North American Academy of Liturgy, Johnson repeated these criticisms in his vice presidential address of 2014,[47] as Edward Foley had in receiving the Berakah award from the same academy the previous year.[48] Foley, a Capuchin and Catholic priest, is the Duns Scotus Professor of Spirituality and Professor of Liturgy and Music at Catholic Theological Union.

Bishop Donald Trautman of Erie, former chair of the bishops' liturgy committee, wrote that translations require broad consultation, but *LA* "has missed a great opportunity to profit from such a collegial and collaborative effort."[49] Instead, it has adopted a "micromanagement style."

After decades of battles over liturgical translations, the CDWDS was asserting its central authority over the words of the Mass, even in the vernacular translations of the world. The strong reaction from liturgists both inside and outside Roman Catholicism shows the broad ownership that academics felt to the words of the Catholic Mass.

Redemptionis Sacramentum

Once the task of retranslating the Missal was in the hands of a regrouped and redirected ICEL, the CDWDS turned its attention to rubrics. The prefect, Cardinal Francis Arinze, released an instruction on matters "to be observed or to be avoided" in the celebration of the Eucharist. The instruction opens with a theological and hierarchical framework, and then strikes this tone: "It is not possible to be silent about the abuses, even quite grave ones, against the nature of the Liturgy and the Sacraments as well as the tradition and the authority of the Church, which in our day not infrequently plague liturgical celebrations in one ecclesial environment or another. In some places the perpetration of liturgical abuses has become almost habitual, a fact which obviously cannot be allowed and must cease" (4).[50]

No one should "here or there alter or vary at will the texts of the Sacred Liturgy" (59). Laypersons and seminarians are not allowed to preach (66). Offerings "may also include gifts given by the faithful in the form of money or other things for the sake of charity toward the poor"; however, "Except for money and occasionally a minimal symbolic portion of other gifts, it is preferable that such offerings be made outside the celebration of Mass" (70). The breaking of the bread "should be brief. The abuse that has prevailed in some places, by which this rite is unnecessarily prolonged and given undue emphasis, with laypersons also helping in contradiction to the norms, should be corrected with all haste" (73). "First Communion should always be administered by a Priest and never outside the celebration of Mass" (87). And so on.

At the time, the Vatican was centralizing words, movements, attitudes, and procedures.

The Sign of Peace

Without a hint of irony, there is plenty of legislation restricting the sign of peace. The Order of Mass presents it as an option. This is probably how it gained sufficient support for its readmission into the Roman Rite after the Second Vatican Council. Some of the faithful resented it, preferring their private space at Mass. Others welcomed it with great freedom of expression.

Some Catholics who have grown to love the sign of peace are dismayed when the priest or deacon does not invite them to offer it. In truth, the rubric says that the cleric calls for the sign of peace "if appropriate." Those words do not appear in the order of celebrating marriage, however, where the same rubric says more directly that the bride, groom, and all present exchange a sign of peace and charity. It is always appropriate at the wedding Mass, apparently, and "all" are expected to participate in it.

The Vatican gathered its concerns in a circular letter issued by the CDWDS in 2014.[51] The catalyst for the letter was a proposal from the 2005 Synod of Bishops concerning the placement of the sign of peace during the Mass. The CDWDS notes, "In our times, fraught with fear and conflict, this gesture has become particularly eloquent, as the Church has become increasingly conscious of her responsibility to pray insistently for the gift of peace and unity for herself and for the whole human family." Still, Pope Benedict XVI had expressed a desire that "this liturgical gesture be done with religious sensibility and sobriety." The CDWDS judged it best to leave the sign of peace where it is, in the communion rite, but cautions the faithful to "avoid abuses such as: the introduction of a 'song of peace' . . . the movement of the faithful from their places . . . the departure of the priest from the altar . . . expressing congratulations, best wishes or condolences among those present."

This largely reframes some legislation from the GIRM, which says that the faithful offer peace "only to those who are nearest" and "in a sober manner" (82). The GIRM encourages each to exchange this dialogue: "The peace of the Lord be with you always." "Amen." In practice, some people may say the first part, but virtually no one says "Amen." Furthermore, in spite of the curia's desire to keep the priest at the altar, there is plenty of video footage showing Pope Francis leaving the altar to share the sign of peace with participants in the front rows.

The letter is another sign of the Vatican's desire to exercise its control over the actions of the Mass. Nonetheless, in the pastoral sphere, the faithful who gather are invited to extend a sign of peace. The nature, extent, location, and style of that gesture is completely and literally in the hands of the people. It is hard for any legislation to control what they actually say and do. The Vatican has the authority, but the people have the power. This is one of the moments when people especially feel that the Mass is theirs.

Conclusions

- Unsurprisingly, the production of liturgical books for the Roman Rite has traditionally come from Rome.

- After the council, the Vatican originally gave authority for vernacular translations to the conferences of bishops.

- The Vatican expressed concern over the results coming forth in the English language.

- Starting with the Lectionary and culminating in the Roman Missal, the CDWDS assumed the final authority for the translation of liturgical books in all vernacular languages.

- The CDWDS made more precisions over the rubrics of the Mass.

- To some extent, the people in the pews who participate at Mass remain autonomous in some choices they make.

These actions seem to give this answer to the question, "Whose Mass is it?" It belongs to the CDWDS.

The 2011 Third Edition
of the Roman Missal

There were two reasons why a new Roman Missal in English appeared in 2011. One pertained to its content, the other to its theory of translation. The change in translation theory is what made the words of the Mass sound different. When people speak of a "third edition" of the Roman Missal, however, they are speaking not about the translation but about its content. The *Missale Romanum* has had three editions now since the Second Vatican Council. Each edition made some changes to the content. For example, the third edition has expanded the calendar of the saints, rearranged the Masses for Various Needs and Occasions, and made more precise the rubrics for Holy Week. Not much of the content changed, but what did change was significant. The Vatican revised its rules of translation just before publishing the Latin third edition. So the same book in English included updates both to its content and to its translation style.

Pope John Paul II promulgated the third edition of the Missal in the year 2000 as part of the celebration of the Jubilee; however, awkwardly, there was no Missal. Work was still underway. The Vatican published the Latin edition in 2002, and then an *emended* Latin edition in 2008. This revision of a definitive text served as a harbinger for the fate of the English translation, which underwent significant last-minute changes. The emended Latin edition (not the "fourth edition") included some minor changes to words and punctuation, but it also corrected some larger mistakes. For example, the first line of the Apostles' Creed is "I believe in God," but the 2002 Missal erroneously had "I believe in one God," which opens the Nicene Creed. This was corrected in 2008. The eucharistic prayers for Masses with children had been included in the 2002 Missal. But these prayers exist in Latin only for the purposes of study. There would never be a pastoral situation when a priest would offer a eucharistic prayer for children in Latin. These are the only prayers of the Roman Rite that can never be offered at Mass in Latin. Since the *Missale Romanum* is not just a reference book but the actual book used whenever the post–Vatican II Mass is celebrated in Latin, the eucharistic prayers for children were removed for the 2008 edition. The original English translations of the Eucharistic Prayers for Masses with Children were later lightly updated and published separately. They are still in use. The 2011 Roman Missal in English was a translation of the 2008 emended third edition in Latin. ICEL shouldered the work.

The Translation Process

The bishops representing the eleven conferences that constitute ICEL gathered twice a year during the period of translation. Seated at table with them were members of ICEL's secretariat from Washington, DC, and other special invitees.[1] The secretariat had apportioned sections of the Missal to a variety of base translators, who submitted their work to a common editorial committee. That committee revised the translations for the sake of uniformity. These were assembled into books and submitted to the eleven bishops of the commission for their review at the meetings. A typical page from the book featured a single prayer; the bishops saw at a glance the Latin original, the rejected 1998 translation, a new base translation, and the revision by the editorial committee, which was proposed for the commission's acceptance. Participants at the meetings took turns reading the prayers aloud, so that everyone could hear and not just read the translation. Whenever an objection was raised, the chair asked for ideas, which were put to a vote of the member bishops and accepted on the basis of a simple majority.

Upon completion of one section of the Missal, the bishops voted on the work as a whole. This "green book" was sent to the conferences of bishops for their suggestions. The CDWDS and Vox Clara also received copies of the work. At a future meeting, ICEL reviewed all the comments to the green book and made revisions case by case. The commission reviewed and amended these, approving each by a simple majority. At the end, the member bishops voted to accept the entire section, which became the "gray book." These were sent back to the eleven conferences for their vote. Those results went directly to the CDWDS. The ICEL bishops no longer made changes to the sections of the Missal after they had approved the gray books. Their work was done.

Not all the conferences of bishops were happy with all the sections of the Missal. Many sections passed, but some did not. For example, the United States bishops rejected the Proper of Seasons at its June meeting in 2008.[2]

Reactions

As the process went along, Catholics gradually became more and more aware that the revised English translation was quickly becoming a reality. In July 2008, Cardinal Arinze surprised the conferences of bishops by granting a *recognitio* on the Order of Mass—even before ICEL had completed the rest of the Missal.[3] The cardinal encouraged catechesis on the forthcoming revised translation.[4]

The bishops of South Africa misunderstood this to mean that they were to implement the revised translation of the Order of Mass. They did so without offering much catechesis and without sufficiently prepared participation aids. Predictably, the people voiced a strong negative reaction.[5] Upon hearing of the premature usage of the Order of Mass, the CDWDS asked the South African bishops to stop, but it was too late.[6] Bishop Kevin Dowling of Rustenburg realized that the reaction from the people required great pastoral care and expressed "deep concern about the hurt and damage decisions like these can cause to the People of God."[7]

Opposition to the Missal's revised translation increased. Periodicals drew attention to the difficulties. *Pray Tell* blog posted a breathless stream of commentary and developments.[8] Bishop Donald Trautman objected that the proposed translations were so dense that they would be impossible for people to pray.[9] Father Michael G. Ryan's petition,

"What if we just said, 'Wait'?" garnered tens of thousands of signatures.[10] As pastor of St. James Cathedral in Seattle, Ryan had submitted his views to *America* magazine,[11] and support for the petition went viral. Ryan's idea was not to halt the Missal altogether but to let some parishes and pastoral centers give the translation a trial run. With practical feedback in hand, a revision could then be implemented with better knowledge of its quality. Even when the final version of the text was made available, objections did not abate. Liturgical theologian Rita Ferrone called it "a translation that is filled with expressions not easily understood by English speakers. It has resulted in prayers that are long-winded, pointlessly complex, hard to proclaim, and difficult to understand."[12]

The translation had its supporters. Over time,[13] some people praised the quality of the work being done, the basic principles of translation, the increasingly evident correlation between liturgical and biblical texts, the theological depth of the presidential prayers, the increased use of gender-inclusive language, the expanded contents of the Roman Missal, the new dismissal formulas, and the catechetical opportunity to present more deeply the meaning of the Mass.

Those who opposed the translation criticized its choice of words that were difficult to understand, such as "consubstantial" and "incarnate." They mourned the loss of popular musical settings of the Order of Mass. They objected to the length of sentences in the presidential prayers. They thought that some lines from the Order of Mass sounded theologically dualistic, such as "And with your spirit" and "my soul shall be healed." Strong opposition formed around changing the words of the consecration from "it will be shed for you and for all" to "it will be poured out for you and for many," which made it sound as if Jesus did not die for all. Many people did not like the first line of the Gloria because it sounded as though it restricted the possession of "peace" to "people of good will." Many lamented losing the acclamation "Christ has died." Others thought that priests— especially those for whom English is not their first language—would struggle to speak the orations in a prayerful way.

Some decisions were outside ICEL's control but caused additional problems. Many objected to the lack of consistently inclusive language and focused on the phrase in the Nicene Creed, "for us men."[14] Many could not agree with changing the word "cup" to "chalice" because of the formal resonance of that word in English and its disconnection to whatever vessel Jesus likely used at the Last Supper. Others did not like the feminine personal pronoun in reference to the church. Many thought the orthography strange—the absence of a hyphen in "Only Begotten Son," the seemingly rhapsodic use of capital letters for some nouns, the appearing and disappearing "O" in the use of the vocative, and incomplete sentence structures such as "Through Christ our Lord."

There was also suspicion about who was really behind the revised translation, as though some conspiracy had formed to undo the reforms of Vatican II. Many lamented the loss of ecumenical involvement in the work, especially in the parts of the translation that were shared by other English-speaking Christian churches.

There are explanations for all of these objections, but perhaps the simplest is that the consultation was broader than most people thought, and the number of those who could and did change the translation was large. Balancing values is always a difficult enterprise when judgment is in the hands of many.

Publication

In April 2010 the Vox Clara committee enjoyed a luncheon with Pope Benedict XVI. The members presented the Holy Father with a bound copy of the completed English translation of the Missal. The pope thanked the committee for helping the CDWDS fulfill its responsibilities. "This has been a truly collegial enterprise," Benedict said. His brief address, however, made no acknowledgment of the work ICEL had done.[15] The luncheon closed with a collect "For the Church."[16] It was the first public release of a final translation of any prayer from the Missal. That one collect included several surprising changes from the gray book translation that eleven conferences of bishops had approved. These redactions to one single somewhat insignificant prayer caused immediate concern that Vox Clara and the CDWDS had made ten thousand changes to ICEL's work. They even changed their own work. The Order of Mass, which had been given a *recognitio* in 2008, had been altered again. No one has publicly accepted responsibility for these changes. The time between the CDWDS's reception of final comments from the conferences of bishops and Vox Clara's luncheon with Pope Benedict, however, was only a few months—not enough time to make ten thousand changes. This raised suspicions that some members of Vox Clara and the CDWDS had advanced their own parallel version of the translation through the final stages of the process.

Before long Wikispooks posted pages purporting to be a complete copy of the Missal that Vox Clara presented to Pope Benedict.[17] Detractors of the translation project found even more reasons to be inflamed. In spite of LA's insistence on preserving the exact meaning of the Latin, examples surfaced where it was not. Some cases of sheer mistranslation appeared. The expansive vocabulary that ICEL favored had been limited. Some elements not found in the Latin had been inserted; others had been omitted. Some scriptural allusions were weakened. Theological problems were introduced. Some grammar was incorrect. Only some of these matters were addressed before the Missal went to press. The *National Catholic Reporter* published a report on these difficulties, purportedly written by ICEL and leaked to NCR's staff.[18]

For example, the collect for the Solemnity of the Most Holy Trinity addresses God the Father with a phrase, "and adore your Unity, powerful in majesty." But there is no "your" in the Latin. It is not the Father who has unity; the Trinity has unity.[19] That theological inaccuracy was absent from the gray book. Whoever thought they could improve that prayer after many theologians and bishops had reviewed it wrote something that the church does not believe. From this and other examples it appears that where LA 20 said that the original words "insofar as possible, must be translated integrally and in the most exact manner," the CDWDS had taken more liberty with "insofar as possible" than the translators thought permissible.

As careful as the revision has been in giving a more literal translation to the Missal, the references to the community standing during the eucharistic prayer have been bleached out of it. For many centuries of Christian history, the entire community stood for the eucharistic prayer, as is still the custom in the East. The first English translation of Eucharistic Prayer II included this line: "We thank you for counting us worthy to stand in your presence and serve you." In the Latin original, the word for "stand" is *astare*. The same Latin word appears in Eucharistic Prayer III, where the first translation had instead, "Father, hear the prayers of the family you have gathered here before you." A similar word, *circumstantium*, appears in Eucharistic

Prayer I, where the first translation rendered it as "all of us gathered here before you," and in Eucharistic Prayer IV, where it appeared as "those here present." Many expected that the revised translation would deliver a more literal rendition of those words, acknowledging the tradition of people standing in union with the priest for the eucharistic prayer. In each case, however, a circumlocution appears. It looks as though the translators did not want the faithful to know the history of posture during the eucharistic prayer.

After the gray books were finished, the CDWDS introduced cognates for words like *oblatio* and *mereor*. ICEL had frequently chosen other words besides "oblation" and "merit" for improved understanding. But the cognates widely appeared in the final book. It is said that one of the main proponents for using the word "oblation" instead of the more familiar word "offering" was Cardinal Francis George, who favored the word because he belongs to a religious community called the Oblates of Mary Immaculate. The English word "merit" sounds like a synonym of "earn," but that is not the meaning of the Latin word *mereor*, which carries more the sense of obtaining an undeserved gift. ICEL's careful treatment of *mereor* was frequently replaced with the word "merit," which unfortunately makes many prayers sound nearly Pelagian.[20]

Some of these difficulties have remained, and they have made the Missal less effective than it could have been. The capricious freedoms of translation improved the quality of some parts of the Missal, but they made the philosophy of translation more difficult to defend because of its uneven application. Nonetheless, every individual involved in the process obviously cared deeply about it and thought that he or she had something unique and wholesome to contribute to the entire English-speaking Church. Lessons, surely, were learned.

The Missal inspired a host of supportive catechetical materials and commentary. A bibliography at the end of this book gives an idea of the range of products available to those facing implementation and needing to explain what happened. Opinions about the Missal divided its commentators into camps as well. More than simply those who support the Missal versus those who oppose the Missal, some chose to catechize about the Missal while others raised a prophetic voice of concern.[21] Prophets raised challenging questions about the process and results of the translation. Catechists helped many people learn more about the Mass, its purpose, the origin of its prayers, and the process of liturgical translation. Some detractors, however, considered the catechesis as so much propaganda.

As a result, some Catholics took the opportunity to learn a great deal about the Mass. Others wondered why fidelity to the Latin was so important. Some accepted the changes without much concern, especially some older Catholics who had lived through the earlier changes right after the council. Many failed to make the revised words their own, working their way through the creed or the responses using a mix of the previous translation with the revised, creating something entirely different. Others who, for example, disapprove of the gender-exclusive language of the creed ("for us men") still omit the offending word and say "for us." In practice, priests too have taken liberties with words that they found too clumsy or inexpressive—as they had with the previous translation in the Sacramentary. Some divide sentences that they feel are too long.

Still, the revised translation has some advantages over the first. It plumbs more theological richness from the original prayers, more biblical allusions have come to light, and the tone is more elevated.

The revised English translation of the Missal, a top-down rather than a grassroots project, uncovered strong emotions about the Catholic Mass. In a world of widespread instant electronic communication, the foibles of people and process were laid bare, and the benefits of the revision were hard to explain convincingly. A great many people discovered within themselves a deep feeling that the Mass belonged to them, and they wanted a voice.

Conclusions

The revised English translation of the Roman Missal uncovered a variety of stakeholders. The torrent of opposition to the project uncovered the strength of feelings that people held toward the Mass. The force driving the project showed the determination of authorities to carry out their will. Both sides experienced gains and losses. Both sides shared a love for the Mass.

- ICEL accepted the responsibility of translating the Missal in accordance with LA, which expressed the wishes of the CDWDS.

- The CDWDS pressed forward with the revision of the Missal, taking some matters into its own hands, revising the work of ICEL and even revising its own work.

- A vast grassroots movement signing a petition to slow down the translation process revealed the strong opinions of those who participate in the Mass and felt underrepresented in the decisions.

- Parishioners, theologians, and bishops all took to journals and blogs to criticize, inform, critique, and praise.

- When the Mass is actually being celebrated, priests and people make some of their own decisions about the words they use.

The question "Whose Mass is it?" morphed into "Whose Missal is it?" Although the CDWDS owned all the final decisions, it met criticism for the way it managed the process and the results it produced. The final book has many merits, but they often went unacknowledged because so many people felt underrepresented in the product. The Mass belongs to all who participate.

Locus of Renewal: Participation

"In the restoration and promotion of the sacred liturgy, this full and active participation by all is the aim to be considered above all else."[1] This principle governed much of the postconciliar liturgical renewal, and its success explains why so many people feel ownership of the Mass.

Liturgical Books

The principle sounded forth from the Constitution on the Sacred Liturgy and found its way into the very rubrics of the main liturgical books.[2]

- At the start of the Eucharist for Palm Sunday, "A brief address is given, in which the faithful are invited to participate actively and consciously in the celebration of this day."[3]

- Before the liturgies of the Triduum get underway, "Pastors should, therefore, not fail to explain to the Christian faithful, as best they can, the meaning and order of the celebrations and to prepare them for active and fruitful participation."[4]

- The baptism of children "should be conferred in a communal celebration for all the recently born children, and in the presence of the faithful, or at least of relatives, friends, and neighbors, who are all to take an active part in the rite."[5]

- The Spanish translation of the same rite puts this exhortation directly into the mouth of the priest or deacon who presides. In his introductory remarks, he addresses the people saying in these or similar words, "Dispongámonos a participar activamente." ("Let us prepare ourselves to participate actively.")

- The Rite of Confirmation notes how important it is for parents to pray attentively: "The duty of the parents is also expressed by their active participation in the celebration of the Sacraments."[6]

- For the Rite of Marriage, episcopal conferences may introduce some adaptations "so as to achieve the conscious and active participation of the faithful."[7]

- The same permission appears in the Rite of Pastoral Care and Anointing of the Sick, where conferences of bishops are allowed to adapt and enlarge the introduction "in order to encourage the conscious and active participation of the faithful."[8]

- When a new church is dedicated, the rector and others skilled at catechesis should explain the ceremony to the people: "Accordingly, the people are to be instructed about the various parts of the church and their use, the rite of dedication, and the chief liturgical symbols employed in it. Thus led by suitable pastoral resources to a full understanding of the meaning of the dedication of a church through its rites and prayers, they will take an active, intelligent, and devout part in the sacred service."[9]

Of interest, the Code of Canon Law of the Catholic Church does not simply require Catholics to "go" to Mass on Sunday; rather, "the faithful are obliged to participate in the Mass."[10] A pastor should also try to encourage the faithful "to practice prayer even as families and take part consciously and actively in the sacred liturgy."[11]

Internal and External Participation

All of this, naturally, has led to a discussion on the meaning of participation at Mass. Some have argued that the council promoted interior participation more than its exterior counterpart. For example, the United States Bishops' Committee for Divine Worship answered questions about Pope Benedict's *Summorum pontificum* saying that the full participation desired by the Second Vatican Council was similar to preconciliar participation, which "begins with an interior participation in the sacrifice of Christ, to which the gathered assembly is joined by the prayers and rites of the Mass."[12] The council, however, never sequenced the two forms. Without explanation, its constitution on the liturgy simply said that pastors should encourage the faithful to participate "both internally and externally"[13] without explicitly defining those terms and certainly not prejudicing one over the other.

In a video message to the eucharistic conference in Dublin, Pope Benedict XVI said, "Not infrequently, the revision of liturgical forms has remained at an external level, and 'active participation' has been confused with external activity. Hence much still remains to be done on the path of real liturgical renewal. In a changed world, increasingly fixated on material things, we must learn to recognize anew the mysterious presence of the Risen Lord, which alone can give breadth and depth to our life."[14] Certainly, interior participation can be enhanced, but it would have balanced the picture if Benedict had praised the increased exterior participation that had come from the council. As the liturgy constitution said, "To promote active participation, the people should be encouraged to take part by means of acclamations, responses, psalmody, antiphons, and songs, as well as by actions, gestures, and bodily attitudes."[15] This they have done.

Nonetheless, it is possible to participate through acclamations, songs, and gestures, without fully grasping the significance of the Mass and what the faithful are being asked to do.[16] The Mass is theirs more than they may realize.

For many Catholics, the high points of the Mass are the consecration of the bread and wine into the Body and Blood of Christ and the reception of Communion. Whether they receive Communion from the tabernacle or the altar does not matter to them, as long as they are sharing in the gift of the real presence. Herein lies the problem. Participation demands more.

The Priesthood of the Faithful

The people are to participate so actively that they are called priests: "Mother Church earnestly desires that all the faithful should be led to that full, conscious, and active participation in liturgical celebrations which is demanded by the nature of the liturgy itself, and to which the Christian people, 'a chosen race, a royal priesthood, a holy nation, a redeemed people' (1 Peter 2:9; cf. 4-5) have a right and obligation by reason of their baptism."[17] The GIRM expands on this theme: "In the celebration of Mass the faithful form a holy people, a people of God's own possession and a royal Priesthood, so that they may give thanks to God and offer the unblemished sacrificial Victim not only by means of the hands of the Priest but also together with him and so that they may learn to offer their very selves."[18] The Rite of Baptism for Children has the celebrant proclaim the same idea as he anoints the child with chrism: "united with his people, you may remain for ever a member of Christ who is Priest, Prophet, and King."[19]

The Sacrifice of the Mass

In the light of the New Testament and the Rite of Baptism for Children, the GIRM says that Christian faithful exercise their priesthood in two predominant ways. They "give thanks to God" and they "offer" Christ "together with the priest." They do this so that "they may learn to offer their very selves."[20]

The Catholic Church teaches that the Eucharist is a sacrament in which people continually participate in the offering of Christ. This belief is not shared by many other Christians, who counter with Hebrews 7:27, which states that Christ offered his sacrifice only once. Actually, the Catholic Church concurs.[21] There is a difference between the historical sacrifice on Calvary and the sacramental participation in that one sacrifice at the celebration of the Eucharist. The Constitution on the Sacred Liturgy summarized this in a dense, careful sentence: "At the Last Supper, on the night when He was betrayed, our Saviour instituted the eucharistic sacrifice of His Body and Blood. He did this in order to perpetuate the sacrifice of the Cross throughout the centuries until He should come again, and so to entrust to His beloved spouse, the Church, a memorial of His death and resurrection."[22] The sacrifice of Christ on the cross was unique and distinct, but Catholics believe that Jesus instituted the eucharistic sacrifice of his Body and Blood at the Last Supper, and that he entrusted this memorial to the church, whose members experience the sacrifice of the cross whenever they gather for the Mass.

Examples of this sacramental participation can be found in the words of the eucharistic prayers. For example, in Eucharistic Prayer III, the priest says to the Father, "we offer you in thanksgiving this holy and living sacrifice." And in Eucharistic Prayer IV, "we offer you his Body and Blood, the sacrifice acceptable to you." The offering of Christ is made not in hopes that God will be pleased with it but with the knowledge that God is pleased with it.

The single word "sacrifice" expresses different layers of meaning. Christ sacrificed himself at Calvary. He entrusts the sacrament of his sacrifice to the church at the Mass. Each person sacrifices his or her own life.

Priest and people have a ritual role. In the eucharistic prayer, "the whole congregation of the faithful joins with Christ in confessing the great deeds of God and in the offering of Sacrifice."[23] Both actions are priestly: confessing God's deeds and offering the sacrifice. Both actions are shared by the priest and the people. The priest has the primary role, and his actions are essential for what takes place. Still, during the eucharistic prayer "[t]he Priest calls upon the people to lift up their hearts towards the Lord in prayer and thanksgiving; he associates the people with himself in the Prayer that he addresses in the name of the entire community to God the Father through Jesus Christ in the Holy Spirit."[24]

That instruction was composed in 1969, and its full significance is best grasped from the perspective of that pivotal year. Prior to the council, the priest and the people both prayed during Mass, but they prayed as if in parallel, not together. It would have surprised the priest that he was supposed to associate the people with himself in the eucharistic prayer. This is one of the most significant examples of the participation of the people. They exercise their priestly ministry together with the celebrant during the eucharistic prayer.

To associate the people with himself, the ordained priest strives to serve as a good presider. The quality of presiding became an issue almost immediately after the Mass went into the vernacular. The new eucharistic prayers were becoming available by 1970. In 1973 the Vatican's Congregation for Divine Worship had heard so many observations about the results that it felt obliged to make these remarks about presidential style: "In reciting prayers, especially the Eucharistic Prayer, the priest must avoid not only a dry, monotonous style of reading but an overly subjective and emotional manner of speaking and acting as well. As he presides over the function, he must be careful in reading, singing or acting to help the participants form a true community, celebrating and living the memorial of the Lord."[25] The people join the priest in offering the sacrifice of Christ. The priest should help them.

The community is not only offering the sacrifice of Christ. Each one also offers the sacrifice of his or her own life. Self-offering is something that people do naturally for those whom they love. Especially evident is the way that parents sacrifice for their children, or that lovers aim to please each other. The same actions of selflessness are easier when done for the beloved than for a difficult person or a stranger. A loving heart lightens the burden of sacrifice.

There are many ways to make this offering. The Second Vatican Council's Dogmatic Constitution on the Church treats this in its section on the laity. Christ equips the Christian faithful to continue his witness and service. "He also gives them a sharing in His priestly function of offering spiritual worship for the glory of God" and the salvation of the world.[26] The First Letter of Peter encouraged the new Christian faithful to be built like living stones into a spiritual house "to be a holy priesthood to offer spiritual sacrifices acceptable to God through Jesus Christ."[27] Examples of these acceptable spiritual sacrifices of the laity include "all their works, prayers and apostolic endeavors, their ordinary married and family life, their daily occupations, their physical and mental relaxation, if carried out in the Spirit, and even the hardships of life, if patiently borne."[28] When they come as a priestly people to participate in the Eucharist, they are offering all their efforts, home life, work, and relaxation—even the patience that accompanies their hardships.

The GIRM includes a chapter on the duties and ministries of the Mass. When it considers the functions of the People of God, it says that they offer the sacrifice at the hands of the priest and together with him. Then, as if to explain further what that sacrifice entails, it says, "They should, moreover, take care to show this by their deep religious sense and their charity toward brothers and sisters who participate with them in the same celebration."[29] One aspect of their sacrifice is their piety, but another is the charity they show to others in the assembly. In almost any group of people assembled at church, there will be some who are good friends and some who are not. There will be some with whom others would probably rather not worship. Yet even in that situation, where people of diverse political, social, moral, and ecclesial views have gathered, they treat one another with charity in the liturgical assembly. That is sacrifice.

The offering of oneself responds to advice that Paul wrote to the Romans: "by the mercies of God . . . offer your bodies as a living sacrifice, holy and pleasing to God, your spiritual worship."[30] Eucharistic Prayer I has a line that expresses this well: "accept this oblation of our service." In Eucharistic Prayer III, on behalf of the people and their offerings, the priest asks God to "make of us an eternal offering to you."

Rubrics

The rubrics of the Mass evoke this sacramental participation.[31] Many fine points are often overlooked, however, because people have remained satisfied with more tangible gains. The priest faces the people; the assembly prays in the vernacular. These two great gifts of the postconciliar liturgy have opened the gateway to participation, but not everyone has stepped through. The participation in the sacrifice culminates in the participation of the Eucharist. Catholics have been slow to appreciate this because of a steady focus on the real presence of Christ in the Eucharist. For many centuries, people did not receive Communion at Mass. The priest did. The people adored the presence of Christ especially during the elevations of the consecrated bread and wine during the recitation of the Roman Canon. When people started receiving Communion, priests often fed them from the tabernacle, not from the altar, as though they were participating in a Communion service in the middle of the priest's Mass. People did not mind. They had come to adore the real presence of Christ and to receive Communion. They were able to do both. But the internal logic of participation, so clear from the rubrics and instructions of the Mass, have remained obscure.

The procession of the gifts comes through the people to the altar as a sign that all are offering themselves to God together with Christ:

"It is desirable that the participation of the faithful be expressed by an offering, whether of bread and wine for the celebration of the Eucharist or of other gifts to relieve the needs of the Church and of the poor."[32] Participation is the offering of oneself for the needs of the church and the world: "[T]he rite of carrying up the offerings still keeps its spiritual efficacy and significance."[33] Yet at some parish Masses, there is no procession of the gifts. Servers bring the gifts from the side table, or the priest retains the preconciliar custom of setting bread on the altar from the beginning of the Mass.

In the rubrics, the priest receives these gifts, goes to the altar, and praises God for them ("Blessed are you, Lord God of all creation . . ."). The following rubric is rarely observed: "Then he places the paten with the bread on the corporal."[34] After praying "Blessed are you" for the gift of wine, "he places the chalice on the corporal."[35] *After* the prayer, not before. This deliberate placement of the elements on the corporal seems to invest them with dignity. The bread and wine for this Mass come from the generosity of the people; these gifts symbolize the participation of the people in this sacrifice. Many times, however, the priest sets the bread and the wine on the corporal before offering God praise for them and then sets them right back down where they were. This gesture blurs the significance of the ritual flow. The gifts are moving from the hands of the people into the hands of the priest. Holding them, he praises God for them immediately, and then, having acknowledged their ultimate source, he places them on the corporal for the forthcoming sacrifice. Even the vocabulary changes. Up to this moment they are gifts; afterward they are offerings. The gifts are freighted by this prayer, and they first go on top of the corporal only after they have been so designated.

The preparation of the gifts starts to unite two sacrifices: that of Christ and that of the individuals in the assembly. Just before he washes his hands, the priest makes a low bow and offers a prayer based on one from the book of Daniel.[36] Azariah, one of the three young men tortured for their faith in the fiery furnace, thinking that his life was at an end, prayed humbly and sincerely that God would find his burning flesh an acceptable holocaust. At Mass, the priest makes a similar prayer: "With humble spirit and contrite heart may we be accepted by you, O Lord, and may our sacrifice in your sight this day be pleasing to you, Lord God." The priest is not literally burning in a fiery pit, but he and the people who have gathered all offer sacrifice in many ways for one another and for many others. He prays that these sacrifices, often made in exhaustion, uncertainty, emotional pain, and solitude, will not be in vain. At least, he prays, may God find them acceptable.

The priest then addresses the people in words that have provoked debate since the revised English translation of the Order of Mass. He asks the people to pray "that my sacrifice and yours may be acceptable to God, the almighty Father." The first English translation had him say, "that our sacrifice" may be acceptable. In Latin, the pronouns are distinct: *meum ac vestrum sacrificium*. The Italian, Spanish, and Vietnamese translations all kept them that way. The French translation referred to "the sacrifice of the whole Church." The German offered three distinct options, one referring to "the gift of the Church," another that eliminates the phrase altogether, and a third that retains both pronouns in the phrase "my offering and yours."

Cardinal Wilfrid Napier submitted his explanation for the distinction during the height of the translation controversy in South Africa. He said that the two distinct pronouns express "that the priest by virtue of his ordination fulfils a different function in the Mass, namely to offer the sacrifice of Calvary on the altar, while the laity are invited to associate their sacrifices—prayer, fasting, sufferings and so on with the sacrifice of the priest."[37] The GIRM does not support such a sharp distinction. The priest is offering his "prayer, fasting, sufferings and so on" as well. And as indicated above, "the whole congregation of the faithful joins with Christ . . . in the offering of Sacrifice."[38] Certainly this is done at the hands of the priest, but the principle of participation is that he does not do it alone.

Anthony Ruff offered a different explanation on the Liturgical Press blog *Pray Tell*: "The Latin doesn't say 'my sacrifice and yours.' *Meum ac vestrum sacrificium* literally is 'my and your sacrifice,' which doesn't imply two different sacrifices. One could argue for translating the difficult Latin idiomatically as 'our sacrifice' (like the 1974 Sacramentary), which is closer to the meaning but doesn't follow the Latin literally, or also as 'this sacrifice, which is mine and yours,' as ICEL proposed and the bishops' conferences approved. But since we now have 'my sacrifice and yours,' which follows some but not all of the Latin, it is important to understand it in the meaning of the Latin—as one sacrifice."[39]

The problem with this interpretation is not the literal meaning of those four Latin words, which can be argued, but their context, which includes the words *acceptabile fiat*. If the words referred to the sacrifice of Christ, it would be presumptuous to think that everyone had to pray that God the Father would find the sacrifice of his Son acceptable. Of course, the Son's sacrifice is acceptable. Eucharistic Prayer IV, as cited above, calls it "the sacrifice acceptable to you." The words "my sacrifice and yours," then, cannot refer to one sacrifice. They refer to manifold sacrifices—the sacrifices that each one, including the priest, is bringing to the altar this day.

When this brief dialogue entered the liturgy in the eighth century, the priest addressed the other ministers in the sanctuary. In the preconciliar missal the servers made the response ("May the Lord accept . . ."), but in the postconciliar missal the entire assembly does.[40] By giving the response to all the people, the meaning of the words "my sacrifice and yours" becomes clearer. It refers not to the sacrifice of Christ but to the many sacrifices of those gathered for worship.

Complicating the clear interpretation of the words is the English translation of the people's response: "May the Lord accept the sacrifice." Latin has no definite article, so it could also be rendered without one: "May the Lord accept sacrifice." This would have broadened the sense of the manifold sacrifice underway.

Rather than asking that the sacrifice of Christ be acceptable, the people are praying that they will be acceptable. To make themselves appear more acceptable, they offer their own lives together with the sacrifice of Christ. As the priest says to the Father in the Second Eucharistic Prayer for Masses of Reconciliation, "accept us also, together with your Son." The priest and people make this prayer as if to take advantage of the Father's good mood.

Strengthening this interpretation is the practice of using incense during the preparation of the gifts. The priest incenses the bread and the wine, the cross and the altar. A deacon or thurifer incenses the priest and the people. Incensation "is an expression of reverence and of prayer."[41] The cross and altar represent the sacrifice of Christ. The bread and the wine are the gifts signifying the sacrifice of the people, who are incensed along with the priest. The sweet-smelling smoke surrounds the gifts, the priest, and the people in hopes that every sacrifice will be acceptable to God.

As the priest and people make the offering together, so they receive Communion together. At least, that is the idea. "It is most desirable that the faithful, just as the Priest himself is bound to do, receive the Lord's Body from hosts consecrated at the same Mass and that, in the cases where this is foreseen, they partake of the chalice (cf. no. 283), so that even by means of the signs Communion may stand out more clearly as a participation in the sacrifice actually being celebrated."[42]

The priest is obliged to receive Communion from the bread and wine consecrated at that very Mass. The people do not share the same obligation, but it is "most desirable" if they receive as the priest does. Communion is intimately tied to the offering. The entire sacrifice of the Mass returns the Communion as the firstfruit of the offering. In the past the rubrics made no provision for the Communion of the people. It was superfluous. All that was needed was the Communion of the priest. Today, though, the Communion of the people is quite common and their participation in the elements consecrated at the same Mass indicates that their own sacrifice shares in the fruits as well. Yet at nearly every Mass, the priest, the deacon, or a communion minister goes to the tabernacle during the Lamb of God to retrieve a ciborium full of hosts consecrated at some previous Mass, at someone else's sacrifice, and distributes these to some of the faithful. After all, the Body of Christ is the Body of Christ. But the sacrifice is not the same. Nor is the participation.

The people should also share in bread broken at the Mass:

> [It] is desirable that the Eucharistic bread . . . be fashioned in such a way that the Priest at Mass with the people is truly able to break it into parts and distribute these to at least some of the faithful. . . . Moreover, the gesture of the fraction or breaking of bread, which was quite simply the term by which the Eucharist was known in apostolic times, will bring out more clearly the force and importance of the sign of the unity of all in the one bread, and of the sign of charity by the fact that the one bread is distributed.[43]

Although the priest is supposed to break the bread "into parts and distribute these to at least some of the faithful,"[44] many priests do not. They follow the preconciliar rubric, which called for him to break the host and consume all its parts. For example, a priest may hold up a two-and-a-half-inch wafer, break it in half, and then break off a smaller piece, which he drops into the chalice. Then, commonly, he places the remaining parts next to each other, as though reassembling the host, and covers the missing part with the thumb and forefinger of one hand. Visually, it looks as if the breaking of bread never happened. He pronounces the words, "Behold the Lamb of God," joins the people in the response, and then places the two pieces on top of each other and consumes them. He drinks from the chalice, swallowing the last remaining fragment. When a priest does this, he does not follow the rubric of GIRM 321. The people do not partake of any of the bread broken at that Mass.

The breaking of bread signifies the unity of the people not only in the Communion but also in their sacrifice. The common practice of distributing Communion from the tabernacle, however, has interfered. As discussed above, there are strong opinions about the location of the tabernacle in a church. Because so many communicants receive from a visibly central tabernacle, they do not make the connection between the sacrifice they make and the Communion they receive. In the minds of many Catholics, the tabernacle is more important than the altar, even during the Mass. The GIRM tries to help: If the tabernacle is placed in the sanctuary, it must stand apart from the main altar of celebration.[45] Furthermore, "The altar should occupy a place where it is truly the center toward which the attention of the whole congregation of the faithful naturally turns."[46] In some churches the cross, the tabernacle, or even the presider's chair is placed where people naturally turn their attention. There should be no confusion between the altar and the tabernacle. But there is.

To emphasize its importance, the altar should be clear of unneeded items: "only what is required for the celebration of the Mass may be placed on the altar table."[47] Furthermore, "The candlesticks should be appropriately placed . . . so that . . . the faithful may not be impeded from a clear view of what takes place at the altar or what is placed upon it."[48] This has become a problem in some parishes where the freestanding altar has been appointed to resemble a preconciliar altar against the back wall of the church, candles lined up to form a backdrop from the perspective of the priest. The GIRM has never permitted it. The altar is not the priest's territory. It is the altar of sacrifice and the table of communion belonging to all the people.

The altar is sacred space. It may be incensed twice during Mass. It is one of only two objects to be kissed. The other is the Book of the Gospels, which may be placed on the altar at the beginning. Both objects symbolize Christ, who is the living stone[49] and whose words are proclaimed from the Book of the Gospels. Some clergy kiss the stole before putting it on before Mass and when taking it off at the end. But the rubrics never call for this, and the stole does not hold the same weight in the celebration as the gospel and the altar.

Ministers reverence the tabernacle with a genuflection only if it is in the sanctuary. They do this "when they approach the altar and when they depart from it, but not during the celebration of Mass itself."[50] No one should genuflect to the tabernacle when approaching the ambo for a reading or entering the sanctuary to help distribute Communion. Ushers should not genuflect before taking up the collection. This inappropriately pulls the tabernacle into the central focus that the altar receives during the Mass.

The only clue about the reverence due to the altar is found not in the Roman Missal but in the Ceremonial of Bishops. It says, "A deep bow is made to the altar by all who enter the sanctuary (chancel), leave it, or pass before the altar."[51] Thus even throughout the Liturgy of the Word, those passing in front of the altar, those entering the sanctuary, and those leaving it all bow to the altar—not to the ambo, the tabernacle, the cross, or the priest. The altar remains the center of focus throughout the Mass. It is the place at which the people participate.

Under certain conditions, the people are invited to receive Communion under both forms. The GIRM calls the practice of sharing Communion from the cup "most desirable"[52]—with good reason: "Holy Communion has a fuller form as a sign when it takes place under both kinds. For in this form the sign of the Eucharistic banquet is more clearly evident and clearer expression is given to the divine will by which the new and eternal Covenant is ratified in the Blood of the Lord, as also the connection between the Eucharistic banquet and the eschatological banquet in the Kingdom of the Father."[53]

Yet there are countries around the world where people are rarely offered Communion from the cup. Although it is common in the

United States, it is by no means available at every celebration of the
Mass in large parts of Latin America, Europe, Africa, and Asia. Even
where the communion cup is available, many Catholics decline. It is
another way that full participation at the Mass being celebrated is
frequently missed. Communicants who drink from the chalice always
drink from the wine consecrated at that Mass, but those who receive
only the host may be receiving Communion entirely from the
tabernacle.

Improving Participation

When asked whose Mass it is, many Catholics have a healthy sense
that it belongs to everyone. Yet full participation at the Mass is still
lacking. Here are some common areas of concern that any parish can
address. Some pertain to the priest; others, to the people. Any one of
them will seem like a small matter of concern, but when considered
together, they show how many ways that people who feel an ownership of the liturgy are not taking it. They are not participating as fully
as they can as the baptized priestly people of God.

Arriving on time. Everyone is busy, but people arrive early when
they are responsible for the event that is underway. The Mass is not
the responsibility of the priest alone. Everyone's participation is
essential. People should arrive at church in plenty of time before the
service begins.

Seats. The front seats in Catholic churches are often left unoccupied
for Mass. If the participants are the priestly people whose responsibility is to offer themselves in sacrifice together with the sacramental
self-offering of Christ on the altar, their proximity to the altar is essential. Those who sit far away when seats are available in the front
simply do not participate as fully as they could. The whole assembly
of the people looks disinterested in offering themselves in sacrifice
when the seats closest to the altar go bare. The ministers in the sanctuary are not the only ones who pray at the altar. Everyone does.

At daily Mass participants commonly scatter to different pews and
positions. The sign of peace may be exchanged according to local
custom, but at some Masses the people sit so far away from each
other that the only way they can exchange peace is to wave at those
who are too far to reach. For a church that values the use of the body

in posture and gesture, the sign of peace becomes impoverished in these circumstances. It is reduced to a friendly wave instead of a deeper sharing of friendship and peace. The priestly people would give a far greater expression of their common purpose if they sat together in the front no matter the size of the church and the number of those in attendance.

At times, people are invited to leave their seats to join a procession, such as on Palm Sunday of the Lord's Passion and the Easter Vigil. Some people would rather not bother, but full, conscious, active participation expects more of them.

Candlesticks. Lighted candles should be placed on or near the altar.[54] Some priests, however, spread six candles at the edge of the altar closest to the people. They obstruct the view of the participants, which opposes the rule of GIRM 307. Everyone participates at the altar—not just those in the sanctuary. A clear view of the altar should invite the offering of the people.

Singing. People are invited to sing hymns, psalms, and responses throughout the Mass. When they do, they give more of themselves to their prayer, and they support the efforts of the entire community. When people do not even pick up a participation aid at the invitation of the cantor, they make everyone else work harder, and they contribute to a visual image of a church that does not fully participate.

Dialogues. The dialogues between the ministers and the people form one of the singular contributions of the postconciliar liturgy. Prior to the council the dialogues were exchanged among the ministers. Altar servers had to learn the responses in Latin because no one else provided those key elements of the Mass. To encourage the participation of the people, responses to the dialogues have been extended to the congregation.

Nonetheless, in practice, some ministers say both parts. Some priests answer "Amen" to the sign of the cross, the presidential prayers, and the blessings. But that word belongs to the people. Even the amen that concludes the eucharistic prayer is the response of the people. Some priests insist that the people should not recite "Through him and with him and in him" with the priest. They are correct. But actually, the priest is not supposed to sing the amen with the people. That is their response, and it completes the dialogue. The same is true of the memorial acclamation. Once the priest introduces "The mystery of faith," he is to fall silent while the people take up the acclamation. In the eucharistic prayer he is addressing his words to God the Father; in the acclamation the people are addressing their words to Christ. In practice, especially when the acclamation is recited, the priest picks one, and the people follow along. The acclamation belongs to the people, however. It would be better if one of them led it (a cantor or the reader, for example) or if the people repeated the same acclamation each day of a liturgical season. Similarly, after the Lord's Prayer, when the priest completes the embolism, the people respond, "For the kingdom. . . ." Many priests recite or sing the words with the people. But that is their reply to the words he has said. If the priest remains silent at these times, he will enhance the participation of the people in the dialogues.

Other problems persist. Some of the people do not respond to the dialogues but silently let others take the lead. Even when receiving Communion, some do not say "Amen" in response to "The Body of Christ" and "The Blood of Christ." Singing the dialogues would enhance them, but if some people chose not to sing, their participation would diminish further.

The collect. After the priest first says, "Let us pray," the assembly observes silence, and then he recites the collect. On feast days and during seasons this prayer sets the tone for what follows. But the GIRM makes an interesting remark about the silence: "Next the Priest calls upon the people to pray and everybody, together with the Priest, observes a brief silence so that they may become aware of being in God's presence and may call to mind their intentions."[55]

The priest says most of the words, but the people are expected to pray along. In fact, they are to fill the silence with a sense of God's presence and the mental formation of intentions that they bring to the Eucharist. Often the final petition of the prayer of the faithful is for the intentions that all the faithful bring. The rubrics, however, think that is happening at the beginning of the collect.

This silence is another way the people are called to participate. They are commissioned as the priestly people to offer prayers for the whole community. Sometimes the presider rushes the silence, and the people do not have time to form their petitions. Many Catholics do not even know that is the purpose of the silence. When the people observe silence together, focus their hearts and minds on the presence of God and the needs that they bring to the Eucharist, and listen attentively to the prayers of the collect, they are participating well. For his part, the priest needs to allow sufficient silence for this to happen and to offer the words of the prayer slowly enough that the people can hear them and pray along.

Bows to the altar. Ministers should bow to the altar when entering or leaving the sanctuary. The rubric, embedded in a book that few people have even heard about,[56] is obscure. If those who proclaim the readings acknowledge the altar on their way to and from the ambo, however, they help everyone refocus their attention on the central furnishing of the sanctuary, the altar. Misplaced genuflections to the tabernacle send the wrong signal about the purpose of the Mass and the source of the upcoming Communion.

The universal prayer. Also known as the prayer of the faithful or the bidding prayers, the postconciliar universal prayer rejoined the Mass after centuries of neglect. The GIRM states the importance of this restoration: "In the Universal Prayer or Prayer of the Faithful, the people respond in some sense to the Word of God which they have received in faith and, exercising the office of their baptismal Priesthood, offer prayers to God for the salvation of all."[57]

Here can be seen the council's emphasis on the priesthood of the baptized. Far from just a theological nicety, the explanation for this part of the Mass carries expectations. The baptized have the office of priesthood, and they are expected to exercise it. They do so by offering prayers to God for the salvation of all people, even those who do not share faith in Christ.

Within guidelines, a parish has complete freedom in composing the words of the universal prayer,[58] a rarity in the Catholic Mass. For convenience, some parishes use a list of petitions that they have downloaded online or purchased from a supplier. A well-constructed prayer of the faithful will be the prayer of the local church, springing from the needs that the local community perceives at home and away.

The collection. By contributing freely to the collection, people help the parish pay its bills. In some cultures, people assume that the priest personally keeps the money, which is not so—at least in the United States. Some people hold back from the collection in order to voice their opposition to the parish, the pastor, the bishop, or the pope. Some think that they have no other way to voice an opinion, so they give meagerly to the collection.

The liturgy, however, views the collection with a different eye. Because it is brought to the altar together with the bread and the wine, it represents the self-offering of the people together with the self-offering of Christ. As Christ gave his life for the salvation of all, so the faithful offer their lives to God together with Christ. The collection does not relate directly to the entrance rites, the Liturgy of the Word, or the Communion. It relates to the preparation of the gifts. It signifies the people's offering of themselves.

When people give little or nothing of what they can, they offer a stark liturgical symbol. They are holding back on one of their primary responsibilities as priests of the liturgy: the offering of themselves to God. What they put in the basket should represent the sincerity with which they are offering their lives as disciples of Jesus Christ.

Often the parish takes up a second collection for some other need— the retirement fund for religious men and women, communications, and the missions, to name but a few. Customarily ushers take up the second collection after Communion. There is no rubric that addresses the situation, however. More fitting is for both collections to be taken up during the preparation of the gifts, so that all the sacrifice is brought to the sanctuary together. A second set of ushers can collect contributions a few pews after the first set. All the contributions can come forward at the same time as part of the offering of the people in preparation for the liturgy of the Eucharist.

In some churches, ushers take up the collection while the priest continues with the other prayers of the Mass. It is not included in the procession of the gifts but is set in the sanctuary whenever it is ready, even if that happens during the eucharistic prayer. This saves a few minutes of time, but it shatters the connection between the financial contribution and the bread and wine. All of this represents the sacrifice of the priestly people, who are offering themselves up with Christ.

On some occasions, other items are placed in the procession of the gifts. For example, at school Masses textbooks and sports equipment may be brought forward. At funerals, people may process with pictures and mementos of the faithful departed. These are going to be retrieved at the end of the Mass, however. They are not part of the sacrifice to be given away. If students have prepared greeting cards for a nursing home, for example, they make a more fitting addition to the preparation of the gifts. It makes as much sense to take text-books back to the classroom after Mass as for the people to take their contribution envelopes back as well. The procession of gifts is a procession of sacrificial offerings.

The corporal. The corporal seems like an insignificant piece of liturgical cloth, but it plays an important role in the liturgy. It designates the area upon which the bread and wine are placed before and after the consecration. It is, in a sense, the first witness of the Eucharist. Bread and wine should not be placed on the corporal before the priest has praised God for them. Setting them there before the prayers obscures the purpose of the corporal.

Consecrated elements should be placed on the corporal, not to its side. Sometimes there are so many chalices and ciboria that they do not all fit on the corporal. Other times the priest or deacon is careless about where he sets the vessels before Communion. More than one corporal may be used to accommodate multiple vessels.

Some churches leave the corporal on top of the altar all day long. Yet the altar should be fairly bare for the start of the Eucharist. Few people would see the corporal resting there, but it would be out of place on top of the altar when the Mass first gets underway. Its purpose pertains to the Liturgy of the Eucharist.

The eucharistic prayer. To pray the entire eucharistic prayer well demands a lot of attention from the priest. It also requires the attention of the people. The Sunday assembly is filled with natural distractions from children who fidget to adults who text. Everyone needs to work on this in a culture where it is becoming ever more difficult to concentrate on one thing at a time and where multitasking is considered a virtue. Priests who celebrate several Masses on Sunday are especially challenged to concentrate each time on the eucharistic prayer. Many people struggle to do it even once.

Learning about the structure of a eucharistic prayer may help. If people realize they are to give thanks through the preface and the first part of the prayer, make their offering in the second half, and raise prayers for various needs at the end, it may help them focus on their various responsibilities.

The institution narrative. The presiding priest manages the nuances of the institution narrative. In the Roman Rite, this is when the consecration of the Mass takes place. The rubrics include some dramatic elements; for example, the priest holds the bread and the chalice as he describes the actions of Christ. They include some devotional elements; for example, the priest shows the bread and the wine to the people for their adoration and then genuflects to add his own. Some priests increase the drama by looking at the people; others increase the devotion by raising the elements high or genuflecting for a long period of time. The dramatic elements pertain to the consecratory function of the words. The devotional elements pertain to the consecratory result of the words.[59]

The rubrics were minimized after the council. The priest now genuflects only twice instead of four times. The ringing of bells is optional. This part of the Mass deserves reverent attention, but it is not designed to derail the overarching purpose of the prayer. It is a "eucharistic" prayer—not an "adoration" prayer. Its purpose is to give thanks and to make an offering. Many Catholics fixate on the moment of consecration, which is an important part of the liturgy. It is preliminary to the sharing of Communion, however, in which they become one with Christ. The liturgy strives to maintain a balance here. Just as some Catholics perceive that the tabernacle is more important than the altar, so some hold that adoration is more important than Communion. At Mass, however, participation indisputably builds toward Communion.

The breaking of bread. The priest should break the bread and share parts of it with the faithful. He is demonstrating the unity of the sacrifice and of the Communion. If he does not share his host, he is separating his sacrifice and Communion from that of the people, instead of uniting them into one.

The size of hosts. Most people receive small circular hosts. These have not been broken, and they do not even look as though they were. By giving people unbroken hosts, the connection between the shared sacrifice and Communion is difficult to see. Instead, the small hosts reinforce a sense that one individual's Communion is independent from another. Larger hosts, broken for the people, strengthen the sign of unity.

Communion from the tabernacle. Perhaps the most important change that parishes could make is to stop offering Communion from the tabernacle at every Mass. At times, the supply builds up, and common sense indicates that the older hosts should be eaten and refreshed. The most practical way to do this is during the communion rite at a designated Mass—but not at every Mass. Most Catholics come to church to receive Communion, and if they receive it from the tabernacle each week, they will not see the significance of the offering they are expected to make and of the Communion they are privileged to share.

Communion under both forms. People often have the option of receiving Communion under both forms, but sometimes the cup is not offered. When it is, many choose not to receive it. This absence from full participation at the Communion table diminishes the symbol of the eucharistic banquet. People should offer their full lives to God; they should receive full Communion at the eucharistic banquet as well.

In coming to Communion, some of the faithful perform additional acts of adoration, such as genuflecting or kneeling in order to receive or bowing to the cup instead of drinking. They risk placing too much emphasis on adoration of the Blessed Sacrament rather than on sharing the Eucharist.

Leaving Mass early. Virtually every parish experiences this problem, some more than others. Some people leave Mass after they receive Communion. They got what they came for. They see no point in staying longer. Yet their participation with the Body of Christ should continue through the period of thanksgiving, the announcements of opportunities of service through the week, the final blessing, and the formal dismissal. The dismissal is an announcement not just that the service is over but that the people's mission has begun. As they sing, dialogue, observe silence, assume postures, and make gestures together, so the people should leave the building together. It is their way of going into the world not alone but as the Body of Christ.

Again, one could argue that these details are small matters. They are. But the aggregate shows a celebration of the Eucharist that de-emphasizes the roles of all present. Catholics instinctively feel that the Mass belongs to them, but not all of them act that way during the service.

Belief in the sacrament of the Eucharist frames two interdependent eucharistic theologies. Catholics believe that the Mass is their participation in the sacrifice of Christ, whose resurrection they share in the sacrament of Communion. They also believe in the real presence of Christ who can be adored in the Blessed Sacrament apart from the Mass. Yet people do not always keep these purposes in relief. Some see the Mass as a time to adore and to receive Communion, rather than to sacrifice and receive Communion.

This has implications for how people should view their lives outside the liturgy. They are not simply disciples who believe; they are apostles who are sent. They sacrifice themselves to help spread the good news of salvation. They should come to Mass ready to symbolize their sacrifice and to draw spiritual nourishment for the week ahead. They have come to the Eucharist not simply for their own personal benefit but for the benefit of the world. The Eucharist is the source and summit of the Christian life; it presumes a people who are not content to adore but who are willing to give everything for the sake of the Gospel.

Conclusions

Many Catholics have the sense that the Mass belongs to them. They take part in its dialogues and songs, gestures and actions. They hear the word of God, and they share Communion with one another and with Christ. Many are not participating as fully as they could, however. The Mass demands that they offer their lives to God with the sacrifice of Christ.

When asked whose Mass it is, the liturgy makes this clear:

- The Mass belongs to the people. All the faithful have been invited to participate, and many do.

- The Mass belongs to the priest. Because many people participate at Mass passively (arriving late, not singing the songs, distracting others, receiving Communion under only one form, leaving the ceremony early), they hand responsibility to the priest. Some priests fully take it.

Whose Mass Is It?

Throughout these chapters, it has become evident that the question that drives this book has a multitude of answers. Ownership of the Mass ranges from the universal to the particular, from the hierarchy to the laity, from Romans to Aboriginals, from Catholics to other believers in Christ.

The revised translation of the Roman Missal more than any other postconciliar event uncovered a variety of stakeholders in the words and purposes of the Mass. Many people claimed to own it, and the intensity of the feelings demonstrated how important the Mass is.

This is as it should be. The Sunday Eucharist is the single most important action that Christians perform. It expresses faith in the resurrection on the Lord's Day. It sets the rhythm for praise and thanks to God. It provides a setting for the faithful to offer their lives to God. It nourishes believers for the week ahead. The faithful center their lives on the Eucharist, and if it changes, it affects them at the core of their being. Consequently, the Mass belongs to many.

- The CDWDS. Ultimately the words and actions of the Mass are established by the Vatican's Congregation for Divine Worship and the Discipline of the Sacraments. As the official arm of the curia dealing with the liturgy, it is responsible for the liturgical books and guidelines that oversee the celebration of the Eucharist.

- Vox Clara. Assisting the CDWDS for English-language translations is Vox Clara, a committee of bishops and other specialists
  who advise the Vatican on the translations before they are placed
  in liturgical books. Vox Clara does not have final authority, but
  it does have the ear of the CDWDS.

- Conferences of Bishops. When the Constitution on the Sacred
  Liturgy approved the use of vernacular languages, it assigned
  the responsibility for translating Latin to the conferences themselves. Over time, the Vatican assumed more of this responsibility. The conferences, however, still develop the translations.
  They review the work, and they approve it before sending it to
  the CDWDS.

- ICEL. The eleven bishops who make up the commission vote on
  the English translations that others have developed. The International Commission on English in the Liturgy houses a secretariat in Washington, DC, and it relies on base translators and
  review teams to prepare the work for the commission of bishops,
  who then send it to the conferences. ICEL has no authority over
  the final translations. It works for the conferences of the bishops
  who populate its eleven-member commission.

- The priest. As has been said of politics, all liturgy is local. It is
  celebrated in a particular church with a particular congregation
  and presided over by a particular priest. Each priest follows the
  same books as every other priest, but the faithful can tell you
  many differences they observe from one priest to the next. This
  produces a feeling that laws are more flexible than they are.
  Still, each priest takes his vocation seriously and celebrates the
  Mass devoutly. He will naturally have a unique way of saying
  the prayers, and he will develop habits that help him better
  express his interpretation of what takes place during Mass.
  Virtually every priest does something outside the liturgical
  books. Some changes are intentional, others he makes unaware.
  But every priest shapes the Mass according to his own style.

- The congregation. The Constitution on the Sacred Liturgy made
  the participation of the people the cornerstone of liturgical renewal, and it has worked. People take a more active role in the

Mass. Because of this, they have strong feelings about what happens when they attend. Many will tolerate some variations, but not all. For the most part, people have cooperated with changes to their own words and actions. But they feel ownership. They should. They have an important role to play. Some do not participate well because of distractions, inabilities, or misinformation about what they should do. But for those who love the Eucharist, their weekly participation is the heartbeat of their life's mission.

- The broader Christian community. Because many other Christian bodies share the basic structure and content of the Roman Catholic Mass, their members feel a friendship and communion with Catholics. Consequently, what happens in one church has an effect on others as well. The changes to the people's responses in the Order of Mass uncovered a great desire for Christian unity, a desire that the liturgy had been helping to feed. The breaking of this unity caused a sense of loss in the ecumenical community. There are other ways that Christians share their faith—through the Bible, moral teachings, charitable actions, and the advocacy for justice. But the liturgy is one important way in which common faith can be well expressed. All Christians have a stake in the Catholic Mass.

- Musicians, architects, and artists. The Catholic Church has always had a close relationship with the arts. Much of music history depends on church history. Many Catholic church buildings are stunning examples of architecture filled with beautiful art. Those who compose and perform music, as well as those who design buildings and decorate them, shape the way that the liturgy happens. Good music will foster good worship. A religious space will nourish participation. The Vatican issues guidelines for the arts, but much of their development is in the hands of skilled practitioners at the local level.

- Special groups. The liturgy undergoes cultural adaptation throughout various nations and peoples, and further inculturation could happen. Although the church is called Roman, it has manifestations throughout the world. There is always something similar and yet something different in the way that the liturgy is celebrated. Inculturated music, art, and architecture are clear examples of how this takes place. More could still be done. As Pope Benedict XVI wrote in another context, "Let us generously open our hearts and make room for everything that the faith itself allows."[1]

- The Second Vatican Council. The council's brilliance shines far. The gathering was the single most important religious event of the twentieth century. It has established a revised way of thinking about the liturgy that included the participation of the people. Many of the arguments about the correct celebration of the liturgy today make appeal to the council's intentions. A correct interpretation of the council leads to a correct interpretation of the liturgy.

- Publishers. The publishers of liturgical books have an influence over the liturgy as well. They have arranged the appearance of the books to lend solemnity to the liturgical action. They have formatted the pages in a way to make the priest's leadership easier. Although the hierarchy has resisted electronic publication of liturgical books, the practice could lead to enhancements. For example, as mentioned above, shortly after the third edition of the Missal was released in English, the name of St. Joseph was added to three of the eucharistic prayers. Immediately, all the books were out of date and had to be corrected by hand. Disposable aids were easier to correct, and they carry the most up-to-date version of the eucharistic prayers. But electronic publication would alleviate this problem. It would also provide a way to update the sanctoral cycle when new saints are added to the local or general calendar. It would permit upgrades to the translation. Prayers that have theological or oral difficulties could be amended more easily. It could accommodate alternative translations of the same prayer. Some object that electronic devices are used for secularity more than sacrality, and that a published book has a single purpose. Still, like the brain that performs a variety of functions, one device can provide a spiritual framework for all its other activities. The same device can be viewed as a phone used for prayer or a prayer book used as a phone. Not every church has access to electronic readers and to the internet, but for those that do, a revised translation of the Missal could be upgraded as frequently as a computer's word processing program.

- Christ. Although there are all these many stakeholders in the celebration of the Mass, none is more important than Christ. The Mass is but a sacramental participation in his sacrifice. The Vatican approves the books, priests make changes to them, composers add words, and people import their own intentions. But the Eucharist is the Lord's table and no one else's. Everyone else is trying to do what Jesus commanded be done in his memory. He is the author. This should supply challenge and solace. The Eucharist should be an occasion for expressing the highest level of charity, yet it is often a place of great ire. Those who fear that the Mass is changing without their permission have the comfort of knowing that the Mass belongs to Christ. Someone may change a translation or a posture, but no one can change the act of Jesus Christ. It is his supreme sacrifice of love for all of humanity that the church enters each time it gathers for the Eucharist. Each time the faithful eat this bread and drink this cup they proclaim his death. They share his life. They receive his mission. After all, they are all celebrating his Mass.

Bibliography

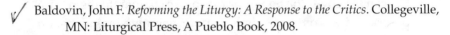

General Resources

Baldovin, John F. *Reforming the Liturgy: A Response to the Critics*. Collegeville, MN: Liturgical Press, A Pueblo Book, 2008.

Barba, Maurizio. *Il Messale Romano: Tradizione e progresso nella terza edizione tipica*. Monumenta Studia Instrumenta Liturgica 34. Città del Vaticano: Libreria Editrice Vaticana, 2004.

———. *La riforma conciliare dell' "Ordo Missae": Il percorso storico-redazionale dei riti d'ingresso, di offertorio e di comunione*. Nuova edizione. Roma: Edizioni Liturgiche, 2008.

Bradshaw, Paul F., and Maxwell E. Johnson. *The Eucharistic Liturgies: Their Evolution and Interpretation*. Collegeville, MN: Liturgical Press, A Pueblo Book, 2012.

Bugnini, Annibale, *The Reform of the Liturgy: 1948–1975*. Translated by Matthew J. O'Connell. Collegeville, MN: Liturgical Press, 1990.

Chupungco, Anscar J. *The Prayers of the New Missal: A Homiletic and Catechetical Companion*. Collegeville, MN: Liturgical Press, 2013.

Craig, Barry M. *Fractio Panis: A History of the Breaking of Bread in the Roman Rite*. Studio Anselmiana. Analecta Liturgica 29. Editions of Sankt Ottilien. Roma: Pontificio Ateneo Sant' Anselmo, 2011.

Francis, Mark R., and Keith F. Pecklers, eds. *Liturgy for the New Millennium: A Commentary on the Revised Sacramentary; Essays in Honor of Anscar J. Chupungco*. Collegeville, MN: Liturgical Press, A Pueblo Book, 2000.

Jeffery, Peter. *Translating Tradition: A Chant Historian Reads Liturgiam Authenticam*. Collegeville, MN: Liturgical Press, A Pueblo Book, 2005.

Johnson, Maxwell E., ed. *Issues in Eucharistic Praying in East and West: Essays in Liturgical Theological Analysis*. Collegeville, MN: Liturgical Press, A Pueblo Book, 2012.

Marini, Piero. *A Challenging Reform: Realizing the Vision of the Liturgical Renewal*. Edited by Mark R. Francis, John R. Page, and Keith F. Pecklers. Collegeville, MN: Liturgical Press, 2007.

Mazza, Enrico. *The Origins of the Eucharistic Prayer*. Collegeville, MN: Liturgical Press, A Pueblo Book, 1995.

McCarthy, Daniel P., and James G. Leachman, eds. *Transition in the Easter Vigil: Becoming Christians*. Vol. 2 of *Liturgiam Æestimare: Appreciating the Liturgy*. Farnborough: St. Michael's Abbey Press, 2011.

Pecklers, Keith F. *The Genius of the Roman Rite: On the Reception and Implementation of the New Missal*. Collegeville, MN: Liturgical Press, A Pueblo Book, 2009.

Taylor, Maurice. *It's the Eucharist, Thank God*. Brandon, Suffolk: Decani Books, 2009.

Turner, Paul. *At the Supper of the Lamb: A Pastoral and Theological Commentary on the Mass*. Chicago: Liturgy Training Publications, 2010.

———. *Let Us Pray: A Guide to the Rubrics of Sunday Mass*. Collegeville, MN: Liturgical Press, A Pueblo Book, 2012.

———. *My Sacrifice and Yours: Our Participation in the Eucharist*. Chicago: Liturgy Training Publications, 2013.

Resources Pertaining to the English Translation of the Third Edition of the Roman Missal

Become One Body, One Spirit in Christ: Deepening our Understanding of the Eucharist in our Lives. DVD. International Commission on English in the Liturgy, 2010.

Binz, Stephen J. *Lectio Divina Bible Study: The Mass in Scripture*. Huntington, IN: Our Sunday Visitor, 2011.

Committee on Divine Worship. *Parish Guide to Implementing the Roman Missal Third Edition*. Washington, DC: United States Conference of Catholic Bishops, 2010.

Denysenko, Nicholas. "The Revision of the Roman Missal: An Orthodox Reflection." *Worship* 85, no. 4 (July 2011): 306–29.

Do This in Memory of Me: Jesus' Command and Our Response through the Ages. DVD. Five Grains Media, 2010.

Duffy, Mervyn. "Revised Roman Missal: The 'Our Father.'" *Liturgy: A Publication of the Auckland Diocesan Liturgy Centre* 36, no. 3 (September 2011): 28–30.

Felong, Kathleen. *Leading through Change: Your Parish and the Revised Roman Missal*. Franklin Park, IL: World Library Publications, 2011.

Ferrone, Rita. "It Doesn't Sing: The Trouble with the New Roman Missal." *Commonweal* 138, no. 13 (July 15, 2011): 14–17.

Finley, Mitch. *Prayers of the Mass: Understanding the Changes*. Fenton, MO: Creative Communications for the Parish, 2010.

Friedman, Greg. *Guide to Changes in the Mass: A Pastor's Take on the* Roman Missal, Third Edition; *Deepen, Nurture, Celebrate*. CD/DVD. St. Anthony Messenger Press, 2011.

Harbert, Bruce. *Companion to the Order of Mass: The New Translation*. Living the Liturgy. London: Catholic Truth Society, 2011.

Hilgartner, Richard. "The Roman Missal: Embracing the New Translation." *Catholic Update* (March 2011).

The History of the Roman Missal. Adapted from an article by Paul Turner. Washington, DC: Federation of Diocesan Liturgical Commissions, 2010.

Introduction of the New Roman Missal: Questions and Answers. London: Catholic Truth Society, 2011.

Johnson, Cuthbert. *A Simple Guide to the Mass*. London: Catholic Truth Society, 2011.

———. *Understanding the Roman Missal: The New Translation*. London: Catholic Truth Society, 2011.

Kelly, Maureen A. *What's New about the Mass*. Chicago: Liturgy Training Publications, 2011.

———. *What's New about the Mass: Handbook for Teachers and Catechists. Teaching Edition*. Chicago: Liturgy Training Publications, 2011.

———. *What's New about the Mass for Teens*. Chicago: Liturgy Training Publications, 2011.

———. *What's New about the Mass for Teens: Handbook for Teachers and Catechists; Teaching Edition*. Chicago: Liturgy Training Publications, 2011.

Kendzia, Mary Carol. *Catholic Update Guide to the Mass*. Cincinnati: St. Anthony Messenger Press, 2011.

King, Nicholas. "Lost, and Found, in Translation: The New English Missal; A User's Guide." *The Tablet* 265, no. 8922 (19 November 2013): S1–S12.

Liturgical Participation of God's People. Washington, DC: Federation of Diocesan Liturgical Commissions, 2010.

Lucatero, Heliodoro. *The Living Mass: Changes to the Roman Missal and How We Worship.* Liguori, MO: Liguori Publications, 2011.

Lythe, Pat. "The 'New' Our Father." *Liturgy: A Publication of the Auckland Diocesan Liturgy Centre* 36, no. 3 (September 2011): 26–27.

Magee, Michael. *Understanding the New Translation of the Roman Missal.* CD. Now You Know Media, 2011.

Magnificat® Roman Missal Companion. Yonkers, NY: Magnificat, 2011.

McManus, Dennis. "Translation Theory in *Liturgiam Authenticam.*" In *Benedict XVI and the Sacred Liturgy: Proceedings of the First Fota International Liturgy Conference, 2008,* edited by Neil J. Roy and Janet E. Rutherford. Dublin: Four Courts Press, 2010.

Mick, Lawrence E. "Changing How We Pray: A Guide to the New Translation of the Roman Missal." *Catholic Update* (August 2010).

Ministering the Missal I. Liturgical Ministry 20 (Summer 2011).

Moroney, James. *A New Translation for a New Roman Missal.* Woodridge, IL: Midwest Theological Forum, 2010.

Morris, Allen, ed. *Praying the Mass: The New Translation of the People's Texts at Mass.* Great Wakering: McCrimmons, 2011.

National Center for Liturgy. *The New Missal: Explaining the Changes.* Dublin: Veritas Publications, 2011.

The New Translation of the Roman Missal: Understanding the Changes. London: Catholic Truth Society, 2011.

Pax Christi Catholic Community. *Lord, Teach Us to Pray: The Meaning and Beauty of the Roman Catholic Mass.* DVD. Collegeville, MN: Liturgical Press, 2011.

Pinyan, Jeffrey. *Praying the Mass: The Prayers of the People; A Guide to the New English Translation of the Mass.* Jeffrey Pinyan, 2009.

Preparing Your Parish for the Revised Roman Missal. Part 1. Editors of *Pastoral Liturgy.* Chicago: Liturgy Training Publications, 2010.

Preparing Your Parish for the Revised Roman Missal. Part 2. Editors of *Pastoral Liturgy.* Chicago: Liturgy Training Publications, 2011.

Questions & Answers about Changes to the Mass. Washington, DC: Federation of Diocesan Liturgical Commissions, 2010.

Richstatter, Thomas. "A Walk through the Mass." *Catholic Update* (September 2011).

Silhavy, Michael, and Lynn Trapp. *New Translation of the Mass: An Educational DVD for Congregations.* MorningStar Music Publishers, 2011.

Sri, Edward. *A Guide to the New Translation of the Mass.* West Chester, PA: Ascension Press, 2011.

Trautman, Donald. "Lost in Translation: The New Mass Prayers May Need Further Definition." *U. S. Catholic* 75, no. 7 (July 2010): 23–25.

✓ Turner, Paul. *Pastoral Companion to The Roman Missal.* Franklin Park, IL: World Library Publications, 2010.

———. *Understanding the Revised Mass Texts.* Chicago: Liturgy Training Publications, 2010.

Turner, Paul, and Kathy Coffey. *Understanding the Revised Mass Texts: Leader's Edition.* Chicago: Liturgy Training Publications, 2010.

✓ Tuzik, Robert L., ed. *Lift Up Your Hearts: A Pastoral, Theological, and Historical Survey of the Third Typical Edition of* The Roman Missal. Chicago: Liturgy Training Publications, 2010.

———. "Translating the Roman Missal." *Pastoral Liturgy* 39, no. 6 (November/December 2008): 4–8.

Weiss, Joseph. *Going to Mass with Roman Missal.* Liguori, MO: Liguori Publications, 2011.

Welk, Thomas. "Translation or Transliteration?" *The New Wine Press* 19, no. 3 (January 2010): 6–7.

White, Joseph D. *Why Is the Translation of the Mass Changing?* Our Sunday Visitor, 2010.

With One Voice: Translation and Implementation of the Third Edition of the Roman Missal. Washington, DC: Federation of Diocesan Liturgical Commissions, 2010.

Workshop Kit for Parish/Liturgical Leaders: Leader Guide. Washington, DC: Federation of Diocesan Liturgical Commissions, 2010.

Workshop Kit for Clergy: Leader Guide. Washington, DC: Federation of Diocesan Liturgical Commissions, 2010.

Zografos, Peter J. *Lifting Up Our Hearts: Praying with the Third Edition of the Roman Missal.* Plainfield, NJ: RENEW International, 2011.

Notes

1. The Mass after the Second Vatican Council

1. Vatican Council II, Constitution on the Sacred Liturgy, *Sacrosanctum concilium* (SC), 4 December 1963: *Acta Apostolica Sedis* (AAS) 56 (1964): 97–138; ConstDecrDecl 3–69; *Documents on the Liturgy 1963–1979: Conciliar, Papal, and Curial Texts* (Collegeville, MN: Liturgical Press, 1982), 1 (DOL).

2. SC 36.2.

3. *Inter œcumenici*, Instruction on Implementing the Constitution on the Sacred Liturgy, 26 September 1964: AAS 56 (1964): 877–900; DOL 23.91.

4. For more details, see Paul Turner, *At the Supper of the Lamb: A Pastoral and Theological Commentary on the Mass* (Chicago: Liturgy Training Publications, 2010).

5. See Paul Turner, *Pastoral Companion to the Roman Missal* (Franklin Park, IL: World Library Publications, 2010).

6. See, for example, Catherine Vincie, *Worship and the New Cosmology: Liturgical and Theological Challenges* (Collegeville, MN: Liturgical Press, 2014.)

7. See *Roman Missal*, General Instruction of the Roman Missal (GIRM), 355.

8. See SC Divine Worship, *Directory for Masses with Children, Pueros baptizatos*, 1 November 1973: AAS 66 (1974): 30–46; Not 10 (1974): 5–21; DOL 276.50–51.

9. Paul Bradshaw, Maxwell E. Johnson, and Edward L. Phillips, *The Apostolic Tradition: A Commentary* (Minneapolis: Augsburg Fortress, 2002), 68.

10. Maurizio Barba, *La riforma conciliare dell' "Ordo Missae": Il percorso storicoredazionale dei riti d'ingresso, di offertorio e di comunione,* (Rome: Centro Liturgico Vincenziano, 2008), 524.

11. For example, see GIRM 79d. The Vatican has affirmed the validity of the anaphora of Addai and Mari, which has no institution narrative. See Robert F. Taft, "Mass without the Consecration?," *America* 188, no. 16 (May 12, 2003): 7–11. Nevertheless, the current Roman Rite completely structures the words and actions of the eucharistic prayer to sustain a belief that the institution narrative consecrates.

12. *Missale Gothicum*, Rerum Ecclesiasticarum Documenta (Rome: Casa Editrice Herder, 1961), 271.

13. The English translation uses "dewfall," perhaps for the sake of aural comprehension, but the Latin word means "dew"—or some other kind of moisture. "Dewfall," which can mean the formation of dew or even the time that dew appears, is less precise.

14. Matthieu Smyth, "The Anaphora of the So-Called 'Apostolic Tradition' and the Roman Eucharistic Prayer," trans. Michael S. Driscoll, in *Issues in Eucharistic Praying in East and West: Essays in Liturgical and Theological Analysis*, ed. Maxwell E. Johnson (Collegeville, MN: Liturgical Press, 2010), 91.

15. SC 36.2.

16. Ibid., 36.3.

17. Ibid., 36.4.

18. Pope Paul VI, "Concession, allowing, *ad experimentum*, use of the vernacular in the canon of the Mass and in ordinations," 31 January 1967 *Notitiae* 3 (1967): 154; DOL 117. See Paul Turner, "An Overview of *Comme le Prévoit*," *The Liturgy Documents*, vol. 3 (Chicago: Liturgy Training Publications, 2013), 410–15.

19. Consilium, "Instruction: *Comme le prévoit*, on the translation of liturgical texts for celebrations with a congregation," 25 January 1969 *Notitiae* 5 (1969): 3–12; DOL 123.

20. Ibid., 6.

21. Ibid., 12.

22. Ibid., 20.

23. Paddy Kearney, *Guardian of the Light: Denis Hurley; Renewing the Church, Opposing Apartheid* (New York: Continuum, 2009), Kindle edition Loc 3364 of 11904.

24. *The Sacramentary* (New York: Catholic Book Publishing Co., 1985), 102.

25. Ibid., 334.

26. SC 14.

2. The Arts

1. SC 116.

2. SC 114.

3. GIA Publications, 2010.

4. *Gotteslob: Katholisches Gebet- und Gesangbuch Erzdiözese Salzburg*, ed. Bischöfen Deutschlands und Österreichs und der Bistümer Bozen-Brixen und Lüttich (Stuttgart: Katholische Bibelanstalt GmbH, 1975). See numbers 456–58, 464, 476, 486, and 507 for some examples.

5. For example, "How Great Thou Art," "On Eagle's Wings," and "Shepherd Me, O God."

6. GIRM 48.

7. GIRM 87.

8. SC 124.

9. GIRM 315.

10. GIRM 85.

11. GIRM 299.

12. GIRM 315.

13. Rite of Baptism for Children 52, for example.

14. Rite of Penance 13.

15. GIRM 318.

16. General Introduction to the Lectionary 37.

17. GIRM 29, 128, and 130.

18. GIRM 29.

19. GIRM 349.

20. http://cathnews.co.nz/wp-content/uploads/2012/04/Ipads-at-Mass.pdf.

21. Ibid.

3. Variations

1. SC 37–40.

2. The Hindu posture would be squatting.

3. If doing so, one joins the palms of one's hands, fingers pointing up, thumbs against the sternum.

4. The gesture is made by placing both knees, both hands, and the head on the ground.

5. The *angavastra* resembles a stole; the garment is worn by some south Indian men around the neck, draping over the front of the pants.

6. The *arati* is a Hindu offering of a lamp or other items.

7. The prayer of the faithful or universal prayer.

8. Consilium, "Rescript (India), on liturgical adaptations to Indian culture," 25 April 1969, Prot. N. 802/69; DOL 43.

9. Ibid.

10. SC 37.

11. Sacred Congregation for Divine Worship, *Liturgicæ instaurationes,* on the orderly carrying out of the Constitution on the Liturgy, 5 September 1970: AAS 62 (1970): 692–704; Not 7 (1971): 10–26; DOL 52.12.

12. CBCI Commission for Liturgy, *New Orders of the Mass for India* (Bangalore: National Biblical Catechetical and Liturgical Centre, 1974).

13. Congregation for Divine Worship and the Discipline of the Sacraments, *Varietates legitimae:* Fourth Instruction for the Right Application of the Conciliar Constitution on the Liturgy (Nos. 37–40), 29 March 1994, 36.

14. John Paul II, "Discourse to the plenary assembly of the Congregation for Divine Worship and the Discipline of the Sacraments," 26 January 1991, No. 3: AAS 83 (1991): 940.

15. Godé Iwele, "Missal for the Dioceses of Zaire," *New Catholic Encyclopedia*, 9:674–76.

16. Nathan Chase, "A History and Analysis of the *Missel Romain pour les Diocèses de Zaïre*," *Obsculta* 6, no. 1 (May 2013): 28. http://digitalcommons.csbsju .edu/obsculta/vol6/iss1/14.

17. This description is based on the article by Chase, with additional information from Iwele.

18. Iwele, "Missal for the Dioceses," 675.

19. Much of what follows relies on the report in Annibale Bugnini, *The Reform of the Liturgy: 1948–1975*, trans. Matthew J. O'Connell (Collegeville, MN: Liturgical Press, 1990), 920–22. Carmel Pilcher also shared her research with the author.

20. *Liturgies and Programme [music]: 40th International Eucharistic Congress Melbourne 1973* (Melbourne: Archdiocese of Melbourne, 1973).

21. See Leo Wearden, "40 Years Ago" in the publication of the Missionaries of the Sacred Heart Australia; www.misacor.org.au/emagazine/current-news/303 -40-years-ago#sthash.88zohASj.dpuf. Photographs may be viewed at that site.

22. Bugnini, *Reform of the Liturgy*, 921. Emended through research by Pilcher.

23. Wearden, "40 Years Ago."

24. Ibid.

25. For an example, see www.cam.org.au/acmv/Article/Article/13140 /Aboriginal-Eucharistic-Prayer.

26. Cited in *Vatican Council II: Reforming Liturgy*, ed. Carmel Pilcher, David Orr, and Elizabeth Harrington (Adelaide: ATF Press, 2013), 61–62.

27. The National Aboriginal and Torres Strait Islander Catholic Council, *Liturgy Resources* (Broome, 2003), 3.

28. National Aboriginal and Torres Strait Islander Catholic Council, *Liturgy Resources, Small Group Reflection and Youth Activities* (Stepney, 2013), 5–7.

29. See www.pastoralprovision.org.

30. The entire book can be viewed at www.orderstvincent.org/BODW.pdf.

31. Ibid., 314.

32. *The People's Anglican Missal in the American Edition* (Long Island, NY: Frank Gavin Liturgical Foundation, 1946).

33. *Anglican Missal* (London: Society of SS Peter and Paul, 1921).

34. www.vatican.va/holy_father/benedict_xvi/apost_constitutions/documents /hf_ben-xvi_apc_20091104_anglicanorum-coetibus_en.html.

35. The ceremony for receiving a validly baptized Christian is called the Rite of Reception into the Full Communion of the Catholic Church—"of," not "with." Ordinarily, Christians outside the Catholic Church do not share sacramental Communion *with* the Catholic Church but are received into the full ecclesial communion *of* the Catholic Church. Surprisingly, the title of this constitution, even in Latin, uses the word "with."

36. *Anglicanorum cœtibus* (Vatican City, 2009): III.

37. See www.anglicanphiladelphia.org/articles/ordinariateuse.pdf. Comments that follow are based on this resource.

38. Introduction to *Anglicanorum cœtibus*.

39. Vatican Council II, "Decree on Ecumenism" (*Unitatis redintegratio*), 21 November 1964: AAS 57 (1965): 90–107; ConstDecrDecl 243–74:4.

40. *Unitatis redintegratio* 8.

41. See www.commontexts.org/rcl/.

42. *New Catholic Encyclopedia*, 2nd ed. (Washington, DC: Thomson-Gale, 2003), s.v. "Consultation on Common Texts."

43. Ibid., s.v. "International Consultation on English Texts."

44. "Presentation of Bishop Wilton D. Gregory to the NCCB," *Committee on the Liturgy Newsletter* 29 (December 1993), *Thirty-Five Years of the BCL Newsletter 1965–2000* (Washington, DC: United States Conference of Catholic Bishops, 2004), 1373.

45. *Lutheran Book of Worship* (Minneapolis: Augsburg Publishing House, 1982).

46. *Book of Common Worship* (Louisville: Westminster/John Knox Press, 1993).

47. *United Methodist Book of Worship* (Nashville: The United Methodist Publishing House, 2005).

48. *A New Zealand Prayer Book / He Karakia Mihinare o Aotearoa* (San Francisco: HarperCollins, 1997).

49. *Book of Common Prayer* (New York: The Church Hymnal Corporation, 1979).

50. *Code of Canon Law: Latin-English Edition*, New English Translation (Washington, DC: Canon Law Society of America, 1983), 1024.

51. Apostolic Letter *Ordinatio sacerdotalis* of John Paul II to the Bishops of the Catholic Church on Reserving Priestly Ordination to Men Alone, 22 May 1994. http://w2.vatican.va/content/john-paul-ii/en/apost_letters/1994/documents/hf_jp-ii_apl_22051994_ordinatio-sacerdotalis.html.

52. www.womensordination.org/about-us/about-our-work/.

53. Sheila Durkin Dierks, *WomenEucharist* (Boulder, CO: WovenWord Press, 1997).

54. Bridget Mary Meehan, Judy Lee, and Dorothy Shugrue (Association of Catholic Women Priests); www.arcwp.org/aids.html.

55. www.catholiccommunion.org.

56. sspx.org/en/about/major-concern.

57. John Paul II, Apostolic Letter *Ecclesia Dei*, Motu Proprio, 2 July 1988. www.vatican.va/holy_father/john_paul_ii/motu_proprio/documents/hf_jp-ii_motu-proprio_02071988_ecclesia-dei_en.html.

58. Ibid.

59. Congregation for Bishops, "Decree Remitting the Excommunication 'Latæ Sententiæ of the Bishops of the Society of St. Pius X.'" www.vatican.va/roman_curia/congregations/cbishops/documents/rc_con_cbishops_doc_20090121_remissione-scomunica_en.html.

60. Benedict XVI, "Letter of His Holiness Benedict XVI to the Bishops of the Catholic Church Concerning the Remission of the Excommunication of the Four Bishops Consecrated by Archbishop Lefebvre," www.vatican.va/holy_father/benedict_xvi/letters/2009/documents/hf_ben-xvi_let_20090310_remissione-scomunica_en.html.

61. "Ai vescovi è stata revocata la scomunica canonica per le ordinazioni illecite, ma resta quella sacramentale, *de facto*, per lo scisma: si sono allontanati dalla comunione con la Chiesa." "I nuovi eretici oggi aggrediscono l'uomo,"

Corriere della Sera (22 December 2013): 5. 80.241.231.25/ucei/PDF/2013/2013
-12-22/2013122226368373.pdf.

62. sspx.org/en/about/mission.

63. www.womensordination.org/about-us/about-our-work/.

64. Benedict XVI, Apostolic Letter given *Motu Proprio, Summorum pontificum*,
on the Use of the Roman Liturgy Prior to the Reform of 1970. www.vatican.va
/holy_father/benedict_xvi/motu_proprio/documents/hf_ben-xvi_motu
-proprio_20070707_summorum-pontificum_en.html.

65. Turner, *At the Supper of the Lamb*, 85.

66. Ibid., 117.

4. The Vatican's Authority

1. Second Vatican Council, "Pastoral Constitution on the Church in the
Modern World" (*Gaudium et spes*) 86c. www.vatican.va/archive/hist_councils/ii
_vatican_council/documents/vat-ii_cons_19651207_gaudium-et-spes_en.html.

2. *BCL Newsletter* 30 (February 1994): 1383.

3. *BCL Newsletter* 28 (March/April 1992): 1290.

4. *BCL Newsletter* 26 (October/November 1990): 1219–23.

5. *BCL Newsletter* 27 (November/December 1991): 1273.

6. *BCL Newsletter* 28 (June/July 1992): 1301; 29 (December 1993): 1373.

7. *BCL Newsletter* 30 (April 1994): 1392.

8. *BCL Newsletter* 30 (November 1994): 1419.

9. For a criticism of the first translation, see Michael J. Wrenn and Kenneth D.
Whitehead, "Unfaithful to Truth: Errant Translation of Catechism Is Rejected,"
Crisis (November 1, 1993), www.crisismagazine.com/1993/unfaithful-to-truth
-errant-translation-of-catechism-is-rejected.

10. *BCL Newsletter* 30 (December 1994).

11. Cardinal-designate [William] Keeler, "The NRSV, the Revised NAB and
the Liturgy," *Origins* 24, no. 22 (November 10, 1994): 376–77.

12. *BCL Newsletter* 31 (March 1995): 1433.

13. *BCL Newsletter* 31 (October 1995): 1463.

14. http://www.ewtn.com/library/curia/cdfnorms.htm.

15. *BCL Newsletter* 33 (June/July 1997): 1543–50.

16. *BCL Newsletter* 33 (November 1997): 1563.

17. Keeler, "The NRSV, the Revised NAB and the Liturgy," 376–77.

18. *The Psalter: A Faithful and Inclusive Rendering from the Hebrew into Contemporary English Poetry, Intended Primarily for Communal Song and Recitation* (Chicago:
Liturgy Training Publications, 1994).

19. http://www.grailsociety.org.uk/who/who.html.

20. The popular song "Three Blind Mice" uses exactly the same rhythmic
principle.

21. www.conceptionabbey.org/news/1-latest-news/459-recognitio.

22. *BCL Newsletter* 44 (July 2008): 26.

23. *BCL Newsletter* 50 (October 2014): 38.

24. Maurice Taylor, *It's the Eucharist, Thank God* (Brandon, Suffolk: Decani Books, 2009), 41–43.

25. *BCL Newsletter* 25 (October/November 1989): 1173.

26. *BCL Newsletter* 32 (July/August 1996): 1503.

27. *BCL Newsletter* 33 (August 1997): 1553.

28. Taylor, *It's the Eucharist*, 45.

29. John Wilkins, "Lost in Translation: The Bishops, the Vatican and the English Liturgy," *Commonweal* (28 November 2005), www.commonwealmagazine.org/lost-translation-1.

30. Jorge A. Cardinal Medina Estévez, Letter of 16 March 2002, www.adoremus .org/CDW-ICELtrans.html.

31. Taylor, *It's the Eucharist*, 57.

32. Ibid., 58.

33. *ICEL Report 2001–2013 to the Member and Associate-Member Conferences of the International Commission on English in the Liturgy* (Washington, DC: The ICEL Secretariat, 2014), 4. See www.icelweb.org/ICEL_Report.pdf.

34. Congregation for Divine Worship and the Discipline of the Sacraments, Fifth Instruction "For the Right Implementation of the Constitution on the Sacred Liturgy of the Second Vatican Council," *Liturgiam authenticam*: On the Use of Vernacular Languages in the Publication of the Books of the Roman Liturgy, www.vatican.va/roman_curia/congregations/ccdds/documents/rc_con _ccdds_doc_20010507_liturgiam-authenticam_en.html.

35. Press release of 19 November 2002, www.vatican.va/roman_curia /congregations/ccdds/documents/rc_con_ccdds_doc_20021119_press-release -vox-clara_en.html.

36. LA 104.

37. Peter Jeffery, *Translating Tradition: A Chant Historian Reads* Liturgiam Au- thenticam (Collegeville, MN: Liturgical Press, 2005), 97–98.

38. John L. Allen Jr., "Liturgist Says Ecumenical Dialogue Is 'Dead,'" *National Catholic Reporter Online* (24 May 2002), http://www.natcath.org/NCR_Online /archives2/2002b/052402/052402i.htm.

39. Cindy Wooden, "New Mass Translation Is Ecumenically Harmful, Anglican Says," *Catholic News Service* (5 May 2011), http://www.catholicnews.com /data/stories/cns/1101794.htm.

40. LA 40.

41. David R. Holeton, "Ecumenical Liturgical Consensus: A Bumpy Road to Christian Unity, Presidential Address," *Studia Liturgica* 38, no. 1 (2008): 1–16.

42. Paul Westermeyer, "An Open Letter to Benedict XVI" (9 October 2009), www.praytellblog.com/index.php/2010/01/13/an-open-letter-to-benedict -xvi/.

43. Maxwell E. Johnson, "Mixed Messages: Liturgy across Christian Churches," *U.S. Catholic* (July 2009), www.uscatholic.org/church/2009/07/mixed-messages.

44. LA 91.

45. LA 40.

46. Maxwell E. Johnson, "The Loss of a Common Language: The End of Ecumenical-Liturgical Convergence?" http://ism.yale.edu/sites/default/files/files/The%20Loss%20of%20a%20Common%20Language.pdf. Also by the same author, "Ecumenism and the Study of Liturgy: What Shall We Do Now?" *Liturgical Ministry* 20 (Winter 2011): 13–21, www.praytellblog.com/wp-content/uploads/2012/01/LM-Johnson-Liturgy-Ecumenism.pdf.

47. Johnson, "*Sacrosanctum concilium*: A Liturgical 'Magna Carta' Then and Now," *Proceedings of the North American Academy of Liturgy* (2014): 9–27.

48. Edward Foley, "Practical Liturgics: A 'Fusionary' Tale," *Proceedings of the North American Academy of Liturgy* (2013): 15.

49. Donald W. Trautman, "The Quest for Authentic Liturgy," *America* (22 October 2001), http://americamagazine.org/issue/347/article/quest-authentic-liturgy.

50. Congregation for Divine Worship and the Discipline of the Sacraments, "Instruction *Redemptionis Sacramentum*: On certain matters to be observed or to be avoided regarding the Most Holy Eucharist," 25 March 2004, www.vatican.va/roman_curia/congregations/ccdds/documents/rc_con_ccdds_doc_20040423_redemptionis-sacramentum_en.html.

51. Congregation for Divine Worship and the Discipline of the Sacraments, "Circular Letter: The Ritual Expression of the Gift of Peace at Mass," Prot n. 414/14.

5. The 2011 Third Edition of the Roman Missal

1. In the interests of disclosure, the author served as a "facilitator" at all of these meetings except the very first ones, keeping a record of the discussion for the secretariat. The role has been largely secretarial, but one of the bishops is the commission's "secretary"; hence, the title of facilitator.

2. *BCL Newsletter* 44 (July 2008): 25.

3. See, for example, *BCL Newsletter* 45 (April 2009): 13.

4. See, for example, *Catholic News Service*, "Vatican Approves New English Translations for Constant Parts of Mass," http://www.catholicnews.com/data/stories/cns/0803857.htm.

5. Michelle Faul, "SAfrica Protest over New Catholic Mass Translation," *Worldwide Religious News* (AP, 17 March 2009), http://wwrn.org/articles/30501/?&place=south-africa.

6. See, for example, Laurie Goodstein, "For New Mass, Closer to Latin, Critics Voice a Plain Objection," http://www.nytimes.com/2011/04/12/us/12mass.html?pagewanted=all&_r=0.

7. Bishop Kevin Dowling, "Why the 'Liturgical Anger' Is Fair," *The Southern Cross, South Africa's Catholic Weekly* (18 January 2009), http://www.scross.co.za /2009/01/why-the-liturgical-anger-is-fair/.

8. For a summary, see http://www.praytellblog.com/index.php/2010/11/06 /translation-directory-watch-this-space/.

9. Donald W. Trautman, "How Accessible Are the New Mass Translations?," *America* (21 May 2007), http://americamagazine.org/issue/615/article/how -accessible-are-new-mass-translations.

10. Signatures can be found at http://www.whatifwejustsaidwait.org /signatures.aspx.

11. Michael G. Ryan, "What If We Said, 'Wait'?" (14 December 2009), http:// americamagazine.org/issue/719/article/what-if-we-said-wait.

12. Rita Ferrone, "It Doesn't Sing: The Trouble with the New Roman Missal," *Commonweal* (30 June 2011), https://www.commonwealmagazine.org/it-doesn't -sing.

13. These next paragraphs are a summary of comments the author heard while offering presentations on the revised translation to a variety of dioceses, religious communities, and schools.

14. Perhaps no one has counted up the gender-exclusive passages of the Sacramentary and of the revised translation, but the Missal on the whole appears to be much more gender-inclusive than its predecessor. The expression "for us men" is identical in both translations. This caused many to believe that the entire revision was non-inclusive. It is more sensitive than most people think, but it missed the opportunity to provide a more acceptable translation for a key phrase at the heart of the weekly profession of faith.

15. "Luncheon of his holiness Benedict XVI with members and consulters of the Vox Clara Committee, Greeting of the Holy Father," http://www.vatican .va/holy_father/benedict_xvi/speeches/2010/april/documents/hf_ben-xvi _spe_20100428_vox-clara-committee_en.html.

16. Edward Pentin, "New Mass Translation Given Rome's Approval," *National Catholic Register* (28 April 2010), http://www.ncregister.com/blog/edward -pentin/new_mass_translation_given_romes_approval.

17. https://wikispooks.com/wiki/Template:RCMissal.

18. "Areas of Difficulty in the Received Text of the Missal," http://ncrnews .org/documents/translation_report.pdf.

19. Anscar J. Chupungco, *The Prayers of the New Missal: A Homiletic and Catechetical Companion* (Collegeville, MN: Liturgical Press, 2013), 95.

20. For help in interpreting the theological concept of "merit," see the *Catechism of the Catholic Church* 2007–9.

21. See Paul Turner, "FDLC: Frederick R. McManus Award," www.paulturner .org/wp-content/uploads/2014/12/FDLC-McManus.pdf.

6. Locus of Renewal: Participation

1. SC 14.

2. See Paul Turner, "Participating Fully, Consciously and Actively in the Mass," http://paulturner.org/wp-content/uploads/2013/08/participation_website.pdf.

3. Palm Sunday of the Passion of the Lord 5.

4. Introduction to the Paschal Triduum 2.

5. Rite of Baptism for Children 32.

6. Rite of Confirmation 3.

7. Rite of Marriage 40.

8. Rite of Pastoral Care and Anointing of the Sick 38e.

9. The Order for the Dedication of a Church 20.

10. Code of Canon Law 1247.

11. Code of Canon Law 528.2.

12. Bishops' Committee for Divine Worship, "Nine Questions on the Extraordinary and Ordinary Forms of the *Missale Romanum*," *Newsletter* 43 (May/June 2007): 27.

13. SC 19.

14. "Video Message of His Holiness Pope Benedict XVI for the Closing of the Fiftieth International Eucharistic Congress in Dublin," www.vatican.va/holy_father/benedict_xvi/messages/pont-messages/2012/documents/hf_ben-xvi_mes_20120617_50cong-euc-dublino_en.html.

15. SC 30.

16. See Paul Turner, *My Sacrifice and Yours: Our Participation in the Eucharist* (Chicago: Liturgy Training Publications, 2013).

17. SC 14.

18. GIRM 95.

19. Rite of Baptism for Children 62.

20. GIRM 95.

21. See, for example, the Catechism of the Catholic Church 606.

22. SC 47.

23. GIRM 78.

24. Ibid.

25. Congregation for Divine Worship, "*Eucharistiæ Participationem*," 17 (27 April 1973), DOL 248: 1991.

26. Vatican Council II, "Dogmatic Constitution on the Church" (*Lumen Gentium*), Solemnly Promulgated by his Holiness Pope Paul VI on 21 November 1964, www.vatican.va/archive/hist_councils/ii_vatican_council/documents/vat-ii_const_19641121_lumen-gentium_en.html, 34.

27. 1 Peter 2:5.

28. *Lumen Gentium* 34.

29. GIRM 95.

30. Romans 12:1.

31. For more on rubrics, see Paul Turner, *Let Us Pray: A Guide to the Rubrics of Sunday Mass* (Collegeville, MN: Liturgical Press, 2012).

32. GIRM 140.

33. GIRM 73.

34. GIRM 141.

35. GIRM 142.

36. Daniel 3:39-40.

37. Cardinal Wilfrid F. Napier, "Why New Mass Translations Were Necessary," *The Southern Cross: South Africa's Catholic Weekly* (22 February 2009), http://www.scross.co.za/2009/02/why-new-mass-translations-were-necessary/.

38. GIRM 78.

39. Anthony Ruff, "Turning Eastward in Lincoln NE" (23 November 2014), http://www.praytellblog.com/index.php/2014/11/23/turning-eastward-in-lincoln-ne/.

40. Turner, *At the Supper of the Lamb*, 60.

41. GIRM 276.

42. GIRM 85.

43. GIRM 321.

44. Ibid.

45. GIRM 315.

46. GIRM 299.

47. GIRM 306.

48. GIRM 307.

49. 1 Peter 2:4; Ephesians 2:20.

50. GIRM 274.

51. *Ceremonial of Bishops* (Collegeville, MN: Liturgical Press, 1989), 72.

52. GIRM 85.

53. GIRM 281.

54. GIRM 117.

55. GIRM 54.

56. Ceremonial of Bishops 72.

57. GIRM 69.

58. GIRM 70.

59. See Turner, *At the Supper of the Lamb*, 81.

7. Whose Mass Is It?

1. "Letter of His Holiness Benedict XVI to the Bishops on the Occasion of the Publication of the Apostolic Letter 'Motu propr. data' *Summorum Pontificum*, on the Use of the Roman Liturgy Prior to the Reform of 1970," www.vatican.va/holy_father/benedict_xvi/letters/2007/documents/hf_ben-xvi_let_20070707_lettera-vescovi_en.html.

Index